I AM HEROD

I AM HEROD

RICHARD KELLY KEMICK

GOOSE LANE EDITIONS

Edited by Carmine Starnino.
"Spirit In The Sky," words and music by Norman Greenbaum, copyright © 1970 Great Honesty Music, Inc. Copyright renewed. All rights administered by Bike Music c/o Concord Music Publishing. All rights reserved used by permission. Reprinted by permission of Hal Leonard LLC.
Cover design by Chris Andrecheck; art direction by Julie Scriver. Bottom detail after a photograph by Litia Fleming.
Page design by Julie Scriver.
Printed in Canada by Marquis.
10 9 8 7 6 5 4 3 2 1

Library and Archives Canada Cataloguing in Publication

Title: I am Herod / Richard Kelly Kemick.
Names: Kemick, Richard Kelly, 1989- author.
Identifiers: Canadiana (print) 20190110368 | Canadiana (ebook) 20190110910 |
ISBN 9781773101422 (softcover) | ISBN 9781773101439 (EPUB) | ISBN 9781773101446 (Kindle)
Subjects: LCSH: Kemick, Richard Kelly, 1989- | LCSH: Passion-plays. | LCSH: Amateur theater—Alberta—Drumheller. | LCSH: Christianity and atheism. | LCSH: Religion and sociology. | LCSH: Alberta—Religion—21st century. | LCSH: Canadian drama—Alberta—Drumheller. | CSH: Canadian wit and humor (English) | CSH: Canadian drama (English)—Alberta—Drumheller.
Classification: LCC PN3215.C2 K46 2019 | DDC 792.1/6—dc23

Goose Lane Editions acknowledges the generous financial support of the Government of Canada, the Canada Council for the Arts, and the Province of New Brunswick.

Goose Lane Editions
500 Beaverbrook Court, Suite 330
Fredericton, New Brunswick
CANADA E3B 5X4
www.gooselane.com

O, it offends me to the soul to hear a robustious periwig-pated fellow tear a passion to tatters, to very rags, to split the ears of the groundlings, who for the most part are capable of nothing but inexplicable dumb shows and noise. I would have such a fellow whipped for o'erdoing Termagant. It out-Herods Herod. (*Hamlet* 3.2.8–13)

PROGRAM

AUTHORIAL NOTE

In the Christian Bible, there are many, many characters —
understandable in a narrative that contains everything from
the beginning of time to the end of it. These characters are
best approached as one would approach a herd of wild horses:
letting them greet and then pass by you, without trying to
hold on. Consequentially, many characters are featured in this
story, but for the sake of ease and reference, I have divided
them into two groups: Those Who Matter and Those Who
Don't.

THE PERSONS OF THE PLAY

Those Who Matter (appearing in order of holiness):

JESUS, the Messiah

JESUS UNDERSTUDY, the Messiah if the Messiah is ill, injured, or
    indisposed

THE HOLY SPIRIT, it's kind of hard to define

GABRIEL, an archangel

SIMON PETER, Jesus' right-hand Apostle

MARTHA OF BETHANY, a follower of Jesus; sister to Mary
    of Bethany (not to be confused with—again, in order of
    holiness—Mary Mother of Jesus, Mary Mother of James, and
    Mary Magdalene)

JUDAS, the Apostle who betrays Jesus

PONTIUS PILATE, Roman prefect who sentences Jesus to
    crucifixion

HEROD ANTIPAS, leader of the Jewish government in Galilee;
    hands Jesus over to Pontius Pilate to be executed; in the text,
    often referred to as, simply, Herod

DIABOLOS, the Devil

Those Who Don't:

EVERYONE ELSE

THE SETTING

Calgary and Drumheller (21st century)

&

Jerusalem and Galilee (1st century)

THE PLAY

ACT 1

AUDITION

‹ SCENE 1 ›

"I want to be Judas," I tell Barrett, the gel-haired director.

"I'll make a note," he says, not touching the pen on his desk, "but right now, I need you to read for Herod Antipas."

I sigh. I am familiar with the part. You send one wrong person to the cross and no one lets you forget it.

ACT II
REHEARSAL

The secondary highway curves against the corrugated hillside, and in the basin of the valley, spring floods have turned the Red Deer River a bodily shade of brown. The current churns through Alberta's Badlands, around the hoodoos and coulees, eroding the sandstone to reveal the spiralling shells of sea creatures.

The river is the leather strap of Canada's Bible Belt. Forty minutes north is the Big Valley Creation Science Museum, devoted to refuting the "lie of evolution"; forty minutes west is the Prairie Bible Institute; forty minutes south is the Rosebud School of the Arts, which may sound secular but in fact aims to provide "top-quality programmes in the realm of the arts to express God's wonderful and universal gifts to His children." And here, in the eight-thousand-person town of Drumheller, the greatest story ever told is being told again.

Early May, and I am driving to join the cast of the Canadian Badlands Passion Play (CBPP). Like most Passion plays, the CBPP's annual performance portrays the life, death, and Resurrection of Jesus Christ. I'm doing this because my own life has become a kind of Hell—not the Christian kind, mind you, full of flames and exquisite suffering, but rather the French kind, composed of unmet desires and existential dread.

A few months ago, I began fighting with Litia, my partner of five years. But our arguments were unlike any I'd known, not brutal or loud but incessant. I couldn't understand how two people who wanted so badly to be kind to each other found themselves doing always the opposite. Afterwards, I often felt that the fights were my fault but initiating them was not, as if I were being governed by some dark master named "Do Not Let It Slide." Who left the junk mail on the counter? Where was the spatula? Why are the scissors in the sink? In the method of a Grand Inquisitor, every question was the guise of a darker interrogation.

"Are you happy?" This from Litia after I had thrown the scissors in the garbage.

"Of course not," I replied, and the bluntness of my answer stunned me. It was like when Mr. Hyde catches his reflection in the laboratory's mirror. Those three simple words at the heart of every tragedy: Is this me?

When you're a child, you imagine life to be something that arrives, like an imperial parade through the gates of Rome, accompanied by great fanfare and endangered animals. But life, it turns out, doesn't so much arrive like mighty Caesar but simply shows up, like black mould, and you're not sure how it happened or when it started, but it's here now and there's no getting rid of it.

By day, I was teaching English literature to engineering students. By night, I was answering their ceaseless emails about what would and would not be on the final exam. The only thing worse than those emails was when they tapered off, and I had to either focus on my floundering writing career — my novella as unwanted as a poltergeist — or scowl around the house, looking for a bone to pick.

As a joke, my friend Peter (who was dodging the marking of his own students' essays) messaged me about the CBPP. "Can you say, Cruci-fiction?" he wrote.

I had never heard of the play, so I watched the promotional video compiled of helicopter shots and smoke bombs, Roman centurions in shining chrome and weeping women in tattered rags, all of it set within a nine-acre natural amphitheatre that seats twenty-five hundred people. The February auditions were just a few days away, six weeks before the semester ended. The music crescendoed, applause thundered, and the video—in all caps—demanded, "WHAT PART WILL YOU PLAY?" I looked down at the dog, curled at my feet, but she was already staring at me, knowing what I was fated to do. Sometimes, I think the only thing that separates circus psychics from the rest of us is that they're not afraid to admit they know the future.

I should mention that I don't believe in God. I don't *not* believe in God either. I'm an agnostic—a term that sounds ancient and mysterious, involving cloaks and candles and shapes drawn onto stone, but is really just an academic way of saying, "Fucked if I know."

Neither of my parents is religious. My mother is too much of a feminist for the Church, and my father listens to John Lennon and imagines there's no Heaven. But when the time came for my brother, Tress, and I to be enrolled in kindergarten, Calgary's Catholic schools had a higher graduation rate than their public counterparts. My folks took a leap of faith and registered my brother and me at St. Boniface Elementary.

In Catholic school, religion was a core subject along with math, science, English, and social studies. When we began sex ed, we would only learn about our menstruating wombs or dropping testicles once a month, but every day would be filled with stories that were too good not to love: stories of oceans being cleaved in two, of oceans quadrupling in size, of a man water-skiing without skis—all of it untarnished by a basic understanding of Newtonian physics. Friday morning, all students were marched into the gymnasium to sing hymns to the Lord. Everyone sang at a mumbling minimum for fear of reproach from the jaded grade sixes, giving each song the sonic quality of a Gregorian chant. Everyone, save me. I sat erect, crosslegged, and as my classmates looked on with derision, I sang loudly—"Yahweh, I know you are near"—my heart brimming with a love so large I couldn't understand it.

I signed up for the Passion play because I wanted to remind myself of religion, to wander back to the borderlands of belief. Because I missed not just faith but the act of it: the camaraderie, the structure, the weekly assurances that happiness is only a ceased heartbeat away. But how to admit this to my friends, my family—all of whom are stylishly secular? More importantly, how to admit to myself that I get so inexplicably sad sometimes that I have reverted to wanting an imaginary friend?

Chronicling my participation in the CBPP would be the perfect guise, a flawless veneer of journalistic objectivity. "I'm only doing this to write about it," I said yesterday when Litia and I went to my parents' house for dinner.

"Just don't come back born-again," my mother replied, and I started to laugh until I realized no one else was.

I enter the river valley, and the radio's top-of-the-hour news is guillotined mid-syllable. I fidget with the dial, but no matter which channel I'm on, the static continues to hiss.

From the highway, the venue of the CBPP is invisible, curtained off by the canyon's bend. The struts of my 2005 Chevy TrailBlazer hiccup off the highway and onto the gravel as I follow the long dirt driveway to where a lone building squats like a Soviet bunker: the cafeteria. And judging by the moat of pickup trucks encircling it, the Welcome BBQ has already started.

I park beside an empty horse pen, and I am making my way across the lot when I glimpse the props garage. A wooden beam is leaning upright against the doorframe. Driven into the beam's ends are two railroad spikes. A fierce wind descends, dust-devils swirling from the hills, and leaves of rust flake off a half-ton's wheel well. The wind howls, and I blindfold myself with the crook of my elbow as the silt swarms into me and hovers the shirt off my body.

All my life I have been young. But I am no longer. I need to decide what kind of life I believe I am living and what will happen to me after I have lived it. I need to decide if God exists.

The howl whimpers into silence, and I lower my arm to make eye contact with the railroad spikes, which the wind has sandblasted so that they twinkle with sunlight. A line of the poet Rilke's appears in my mind: "Who, if I cried out, would hear me among the Angelic Orders?"

"Hello?" I holler.

From the cafeteria: "We're over here!"

⚓ ⚓ ⚓ ⚓

All Passion plays derive from the Christian Bible's New Testament, comprised chiefly of the Gospels of Matthew, Mark, Luke, and John. But the four Gospels disagree on many fundamental issues. They differ on where Jesus went, which sermons He gave, and who was ultimately responsible for His death. Many Passion plays address these discrepancies by combining all four Gospels into a composite of what is generally believed to have happened: Jesus Christ was tried by Pontius Pilate and forsaken by Herod; Christ was crucified, He died, He was buried; on the third day, He rose again and ascended into Heaven.

When the CBPP began in 1994, the script partook of this hybrid model, assembled with verbatim readings of the New Testament: the same story, the same staging, year after underwhelming year. In 2006 and in response to declining ticket sales, the organization began debuting a new script every half-decade, rotating through the Gospels. From 2006 to 2010 were the wildly adored Matthew years; 2011 to 2015, the slightly less loved though still successful John years. We are now into the second season of the precarious era of Luke, a Gospel that is by far the longest and also widely considered to be the weakest of the four. Luke's is the only Gospel not written by an Apostle; he was a physician and, as such, has the storytelling style of a textbook.

But since the Matthew and Mark Gospels are so similar as to be almost identical (most scholars believe them to be written by the same person), there were no other options left. Because, while every Gospel has its strengths, opting to overlook one book just because it has a subpar narrative puts the entire endeavour in a sticky spot. In some way, the CBPP would be saying not just that their play had failed but that a gospeller had.

At nearly 130 people, the cast is too large for a group introduction, so I spend the afternoon introducing myself. "Yes, the writer," I say. "Yes, the spy."

Most of the actors already know each other, but I am still piecing the cast list together. As I eat the Welcome BBQ's vegetarian option (a buttered hot dog bun, cherry tomatoes, and a side of romaine lettuce—dry, since the dressing has bacon bits), I glance around the cafeteria and wonder if Mother Mary walks among us.

Aside from Jesus, Jesus Understudy, and Gabriel, who receive a modest honorarium, all actors are volunteers. We have committed to a minimum of two hundred rehearsal hours, every Friday through Sunday (and some Wednesdays and Thursdays) from May to July, in preparation for our nine-show run. Hardly any actors live in Drumheller; many are from surrounding agricultural towns, but some travel from as far away as Peace River or Saskatchewan, driving eight hours each direction. Apart from a sizeable minority who are unemployed, most volunteers with jobs must take time off to accommodate such a rigorous schedule. This sacrifice is keenly felt, since the majority of cast members are working class: mechanics and baristas; cashiers and contractors; there is a lumberjack, an office administrator, a bus driver. McDonald's is the largest employer, followed closely by Starbucks; the most common trade is being a professional Santa Claus. The actors are young and old, married and single, urban and rural. But they are all, without exception, Christian—and, as the impromptu prayer session by the ladies' washroom indicates, fervently so.

When I tell people my part, their reactions are uniform. "Oh?" they say, through a strained smile, before declaring a need to revisit the buffet. You can almost hear them thinking, *You're just going to admit that?*

I have been cast as Herod Antipas, not to be confused with the five other Herods in the family (six if you include his wife, named, unsettlingly, Herodias). Scripturally speaking, Herod is known primarily for his craven abandonment of Christ to the crucifying mob. In a scant three verses, the Gospel of Luke explains how Herod had the opportunity to intervene in Pilate's sentencing of Jesus but believed the Lord to be more swindler than Saviour and dismissed Him to execution.[1]

But, as I often tell my elderly neighbour, just because something is old doesn't make it right—and the Bible is no different. According to several scholarly biographies, Herod was a successful economist, diplomat, and urban planner. After an early divorce, he was uxoriously married to Herodias for forty years; this in contrast to his father's unending harem of wives. He survived his usurping siblings, the blood-lusty Roman emperors, and invasions by foreign empires. But instead of being remembered for any of this, he is one of the most slandered figures in Scripture (which is saying quite a bit considering the Bible's cast includes, namely, the Devil). Herod is the Bond villain of the New Testament: shrewd yet inept, salacious yet infertile. He is so repulsive that he is the only character loathed by both Pontius Pilate *and* Jesus. He is the algae on river rocks, the Tupperware in a lost-and-found, the drain in a public shower. And, for the rest of the summer, he will be me.

A woman who will play Baptizee 4 is showing off her new purse sewn of zebra skin—the mane forming part of the clasp. As I reach out to compliment the softness of the striped leather, someone nearby tells her my role. Aghast, she clutches the purse to her chest. She then turns to her neighbour and starts a conversation about how

---

1   For the sake of comparison, Luke dedicates the same number of verses on explicating the taxation policies of ancient Rome (Luke 2:1–3).

homosexuals who use the symbol of the rainbow are unwittingly using the symbol of God's judgement. "Remember the flood?" she tells Blind Woman. "Remember the Great Flood?"

I find another seat at the opposite end of the building, beside a man with a navel-length beard and a young woman with hair the colour of a burning bush. She tells him that she is Martha of Bethany, the sister of Lazarus, whom Jesus resurrects from the dead. "But," Martha of Bethany says, "my sister got the Holy Spirit."

The man nods and combs his fingers through his beard. "Roles come to those who need them."

Martha of Bethany leaves to get another hot dog. The man turns to me and asks, "Where do you locate your faith?"

After Jesus' arrest, Simon Peter thrice denied having a relationship with Christ. But all was forgiven, and Simon Peter went on to guard the gates of Heaven. So on the drive here, I made a deal with myself that I could thrice *profess* having a relationship with Christ without there being any lasting repercussions.

I use my first lie by telling a half-truth. "I went to Catholic school."

"I'm Catholic too," he says, and his face blooms like a cactus flower.

I point to the script. "Who are you?"

"Diabolos," he responds, and the bloom closes, his eyes pointed and hard and studying my face. "Have we met before?"

⚒ ⚒ ⚒ ⚒

The history of the modern Passion play begins in 1634. According to legend, the bubonic plague was blackening the German countryside, and the Bavarian town of Oberammergau pledged to enact the life, Crucifixion, and Resurrection of Christ once every ten years if they were spared. As divine intervention would have it, sickness skipped over the thespians, and Passion plays were soon seen as a way to court favour with the Lord and became a bit of a plague themselves, outbreaking all over the globe.

Just a few decades ago, Passion plays were ubiquitous throughout Western culture, their popularity culminating in Andrew Lloyd Webber's 1973 rock opera, *Jesus Christ Superstar*. There are, however, fundamental differences between the CBPP's production and Lloyd Webber's. *Jesus Christ Superstar* does not express fidelity to any one Gospel and claims artistic freedom to invent as much history and theology as necessary; nowhere in the Bible does it state the Apostles defended Mary Magdalene, or Pontius Pilate was clairvoyant, or that Judas outran a tank. Most importantly, the film does not depict the Resurrection. *Jesus Christ Superstar* is to Passion plays what Santa Claus is to Christmas: profitable, palpable, and having absolutely nothing to do with salvation. But in some ways, the success of *Jesus Christ Superstar* was the death blow for commercial Passion plays. The rock opera became the definitive version of the story, damning almost all other productions to the church basement.

But the CBPP is not a Sunday school affair. Rather, it has an annual operating budget of nearly a million dollars, is one of the province's main attractions, and routinely features upwards of a hundred human actors and a handful of animal ones (horses, dogs, sheep, etc.). The aesthetic quality of the play rivals the continent's grandest theatre festivals, garnering tourist awards and government grants. An individual show has the running cost of nearly $100,000 and is performed on the country's largest stage, an outdoor amphitheatre where over fifteen thousand people sit per season. But while the expense of each season has never been higher, interest has cratered.

By most accounts, last season's production was a Chernobylian meltdown: ticket sales were devastatingly low, and the company plunged into debt. In response, nearly the entire directing team was fired; dozens of veteran volunteer actors have not returned; most notably, preseason ticket sales have shrivelled up like a corpse left in the sun.

When I spoke on the phone with Vance, the CBPP's executive director, and pitched him the idea of me writing about the play, he said, "You're doing this just in time. This may be our last year. If we don't come through big—and I mean *big*—we're done for."

The CBPP is broke, and it's not just money they're short on.

Every Passion play demands a large cast. Right off the top, you need thirteen actors to play Jesus and His twelve Apostles. Double-casting is impossible since they all must be onstage at the same time. Then there is the Virgin Mary (the Lord's mother) and Mary Magdalene (the Lord's lady-love). Double-casting these roles is technically possible but is discouraged because of the Freudian connotations. Finally, there are all the periphery characters who are no less integral: Pontius Pilate, some Pharisees (the upper echelons of Jewish society), a handful of Roman soldiers, some weeping women, enough Villagers to get a good mob going, and Herod—me. By this point, most scripts will double that of *Les Misérables* in number of actors and sustained periods of suffering.

However, unlike most other Passion plays, the CBPP not only depicts the trial, Crucifixion, and Resurrection of Jesus but showcases His entire life. This breadth gets even broader since our script is based on the Gospel of Luke, which describes both the birth of Christ and the birth of time itself, from Creation onwards, meaning a near infinite number of actors is needed. Admittedly, most of these characters mean nothing. They appear randomly and without backstory, disappearing with equal promptness, as in a story told by a toddler. But they exist nonetheless, and to erase a name from the script is to erase it from the Book of Life.

For the last few years, the CBPP has been struggling with the recruitment of its volunteer cast, and this season—its twenty-fourth—has been particularly hard. In the months between audition and rehearsal, we have been routinely bombarded with "recruit your congregation" emails. Actors have been urged to bring friends to the Welcome BBQ where, under the ploy of free food, they are coerced into auditioning. To entice even more interest, an announcement was leaked that our fresh, famous, and prodigiously talented Jesus has been brought in from Vancouver, accompanied by His own IMDb page, which includes a credit guest-starring on the hit American television show *Supernatural*. But despite all this, our patriarchal script remains starved for male actors, with some men playing upwards of six characters.

I take it as a compliment that Herod is so important that I have only the one role. But my table does not take it this way. Everyone stops chewing, frozen, forks in mid-air. Everyone except one woman who clasps her hands and says, "I'm your advisor!"

Technically, her role is "Herod *Attendant*" (emphasis mine) but, not liking the part, she has promoted herself. She admits that there will be no changing of her lines (of which she has none) or even costume, just her general poise onstage. Her alteration to the script strikes me as odd not only because of its invisibility but because of her presumed connection between her character—however inconsequential—and herself.

She introduces me to the rest of the table. I am dining with Moses, John the Baptist, Midwife 2, Beggar Woman, and a Dark Angel. She then nods towards a man working his way through a pyramid of hot dogs, each one ingested in two efficient bites.

"He's Simon Peter," Herod's Advisor whispers. I extend my hand to him, and he shakes it with his right while continuing to eat with his left.

Beggar Woman asks how I envision Herod, but before I can respond, Simon Peter says, "Herod is a snivelling, spoiled little brat."

Everyone in the cafeteria laughs. A Pharisee actually claps.

I excuse myself to the washroom, side-stepping the prayer session that still loiters in front of the ladies'.

Inside, I stare at the mirror. "Stupid Simon Peter," I say. "How many countries do *you* run?"

Technically speaking, Herod Antipas didn't run any countries either. His father, Herod the Great, was a client king of Rome and governed Judea, a territory that corresponds roughly to modern-day Israel. Herod the Great was a military tactician who single-handedly forged a new aristocracy and has been called one of civilization's greatest builders. But for all of the deeds Herod the Great accomplished, he is most remembered for the one he didn't. When he heard that the King of the Jews had been born (a title which he himself currently held), he ordered all of Bethlehem's male babies to be murdered. But because an angel appeared to Christ's stepfather, Joseph, in a dream, the baby Jesus escaped this slaughter. Unfortunately, however, no one else had such forewarning, and uncountable infants were executed.[2]

From five different wives, Herod the Great had eleven sons, seven of whom were — at some point — chosen over Herod Antipas to be heir. Herod Antipas only rose through the ranks because his brothers kept on trying to murder their father in such outlandish ways that the plots read like bad theatre. Upon Herod the Great's death, Emperor Augustus appointed three brothers to inherit their father's kingdom: Archelaus to govern Judea, the profitable half of the empire; Philip to govern the northeastern quarter and link to Rome; and lowly Herod Antipas, whose defining skill was his sheer unwillingness to try and kill his father, would govern the provinces of Galilee and Perea, not as king but as tetrarch, a regional position assigned at the discretion of the emperor.

The runt of the litter, the half-breed, living in the shadow of a father whose greatness was literally his last name. But unlike my dad, I actually killed Christ. So at least there's that.

ਧ ਧ ਧਧ

By the time we leave the Welcome BBQ, the sky is dark, and the Milky Way gleams like an overhead city. The stars of the show (Jesus, Jesus Understudy, and Gabriel) are given private trailers on-site, but the rest of the cast stays fifteen minutes west in an abandoned baseball diamond converted into a campground.

Aside from one bus-sized RV—in which the disciple Cleopas lives year-round—most trailers are small and weathered, with mascara-

---

2   By coincidence, the Church commemorates this day, named the Massacre of the Innocents, on my birthday (December 28).

runs of rust beneath each window. I have erected my tent in a corner of a field known as Tent City. Extension cords snake through the grass, weaving their way beneath tarps to power heaters or air pumps. To my left is a tent replete with a garden of solar lights circling the pegs. To my right is a tent that could have belonged to the original Wise Men: white canvas towers with stencils of candelabras along their steepled tops. Home-schooled teenagers swoop between the trees, shrill with excitement, while groups of bearded men laugh loudly and their nearby wives shake their heads and giggle among themselves.

I recently asked a friend if she believed in God. "I'm not religious, but I'm spiritual," she replied, echoing the theological catchphrase of our age.

"What does that even mean?"

"It means," she said, "it's too restrictive to believe in a church but too terrifying to believe in nothing."

And while I pretended not to understand, I did. There's something about the mythology that's so hard to let go. How lonely everything becomes when you know everything that exists.

In my tent, I hear Martha of Bethany telling someone, "This is going to be a life-changing summer."

"Life-changing," her friend agrees.

But a third says, "Easy for you two to say. I'm only an angel."

I can tell by the sound of their feet on the grass that they have stopped walking. Martha of Bethany says, "Roles come to those who need them."

I fall asleep to the sound of the Red Deer River, the water running atop skulls of prehistoric size, the dragons who never made it onto the ark, who remember the Great Flood.

‹ SCENE 2 ›

Catholic junior high was different from Catholic elementary. Gone were the stories of plunging tragedy and vaulting victory, of a dove landing within an old man's hands and a boy living among the lions. In their place were the priestly assurances that our lust-riddled bodies were, without exception, going to burn. Not that any of us were having sex, but Father Bill knew we were doing the next-best thing. "Your body is not made for your own pleasure," he would bellow each sermon, "but for the pleasure of the Lord," to which my best friend, Jason D'Souza, replied, "Sicko," and was promptly told to sit outside.

It wasn't that we objected to the conservatism of the Church; by some stroke of fortune, the sexist, homophobic European-elitism lined up quite nicely with the world view of a thirteen-year-old boy. What we objected to was the boredom. Our calendars were filled with exams on the Song of Solomon, quizzes on Israeli geography, and short-answer questions on the architectural construction of Heaven.[3]

But before my last year of junior high, in the midst of my fall from grace, I had a summer of being saved. My mother was looking for summer camps to send my brother and me to. Tress wanted to go somewhere with a lake; I wanted to go somewhere with horses; my father wanted us to go somewhere far enough away that we couldn't be picked up early (I had a congenital case of homesickness). No single camp fulfilled all of these desires, so my mother found one for Tress in the south of the province and one for me in the west.

During my first day at Camp Evergreen, after introducing ourselves to our cabinmates and participating in a camp-wide watermelon

---

3   Which, for the record, is a square-shaped city with walls of jasper measuring roughly 2,200 kilometres each (Revelation 21:10–27).

eating contest (in which I placed third), we were given our schedules for the week.

"What's this Worship block?" I asked my counsellor, a man with a soul patch.

"Prayer service," he responded.

Horseback riding was programmed every other day, but Worship (the only activity to be capitalized) was scheduled each day after breakfast, lunch, dinner, and evening snack, with a quick top-up before bed. "Five fucking times a day?" I said.

My counsellor gnawed on his soul patch. "You know," he said, "each swear sours your heart to God."

Frankly, I did not know what this meant. Just as my mother hadn't known this was a Baptist camp. Most likely, she had simply assumed the pamphlet's designer had a penchant for doves. Though what I did know was that I would not be picked up early.

But it turned out I loved Worship, even more than horseback riding. The service was led by a pastor-cum-magician who would contort the day's moral into his various tricks.

"And just like I knew Samantha's card was the seven of spades, the Lord Jesus Christ knows your heart. All you have to do is let Him build a house there, let Him become—" and from behind Samantha's ear he pulled another card "—your King of Hearts."

Everyone gasped, Samantha clutched her chest, and an electric guitar kicked in. The pastor raised his hands in the air. "Let us praise His name," he said, and my counsellor stood and turned his head to the ceiling, tears trickling from the corners of his eyes, his soul patch pointing heavenwards.

Over the course of my two weeks at Camp Evergreen, I too would raise my hands in the air (one at first, then both), and take "chat sessions" called "Evolution or Absolution?" "Dating with God," and "Sing-Along Psalms" (guitars provided). I also took a pottery class during which the shapely instructor with the plunging necklines would remind us that "we, too, were made from clay."

Back in Calgary, Tress told me that he learned how to snorkel, kayak, and wakeboard.

"Well," I replied, "I learned how to praise His name."

For the most part, my religiosity revolved around listening to Christian rock, chastising my friends who shoplifted, and telling my parents they should have given Tress a Biblical name. I also spent a large amount of time touching up my permanent-marker soul patch.

September arrived, I started grade nine, and—to my own surprise—I stuck with Christ. I adopted this sheepish and half-high look, something I thought a prophet would have, and led Worship from the second row of the bleachers. The students who gathered were a boy who was home-schooled half the year, a girl with a harelip, a recent Polish immigrant, and a set of fraternal twins who appeared to be romantically involved. I didn't know what to preach, and I didn't know any magic tricks, so my sermons were mostly composed of abstract phrases like "sing the spirit" and "hear the thoughts of Heaven."

"And now," I said, "let us praise His name," and even the lovelorn twins would be moved to such spirituality that they would momentarily break their hand-holding to present their palms to Heaven.

I stayed with God for over six months but less than twelve. What was it that broke me? Swearing. I missed it so much. Just listen to the words: *Asshole. Bastard. Son of a bitch.* And then there are the words unique to a junior high school boy, the ones with their own raw beauty. *Shit tits. Fishfucker. Front-gut-butt-cunt. Goddamn.* And with that last one in particular, the forbidden luxury of when you split it in two: *God. Damn.* Each word like the burst of biting into a fresh lime.

Once I broke the second commandment, it was easy to play fast and loose with the following eight. Don't get me wrong, I've yet to murder anyone, but I'll covet what I want to covet. And once I parted ways with the latter nine, it was only a matter of time before I parted ways with the first.

At the end of grade nine, I was asked to give the opening prayer at our graduation mass. The fact that I was asked to do this shows nothing of my own devotion but rather how shallow a pool Father Bill had to draw from. As the prayer meandered forward, I glanced up into the audience of parents. In the candlelight, I could see their eyes glaze over. And I was struck with the understanding that no one actually cared, that we were all so bored with what we believed.

I started making cuts. Father Bill, who was sitting on the stage nearby, was familiar with the prayer's unedited version and his face reddened. But for the first time in our years together, he was powerless.

A few weeks prior, I had been accepted into a fine arts public school. My grade nine graduation was to be the last time I could enter a church without feeling like a fraud. And as I skipped the last five lines of the prayer, I didn't realize I was on the cusp of losing a tiny part of myself. Sure, it was the part I most despised and was embarrassed by, but if we start kicking those parts of ourselves to the curb, won't we soon be as boring as the saints?

‹ SCENE 3 ›

The morning of our first rehearsal, I pour myself a coffee in the campground's decommissioned food truck, which acts as our kitchen and is lit with a night-light Jesus. Outside, I join a small group of chatting millennials. Their conversation seems charged, but when I enter their circle, they stop.

"Where are the showers?" I ask, and Widow with Two Pennies points me to a renovated shipping container.

As I leave their circle, Andrew the Apostle continues the conversation. "But what I'm saying," he tells Widow with Two Pennies, "is if you really needed a part-time job, the Lord would have given you one by now."

At ten a.m., the day begins, and I see the stage for the first time. When I originally told Litia about the play, she assumed it was some bathrobe-and-fake-beard production. "You're all wrong," I said, showing her the website's photographs: the stage combat, the chariot races, the startlingly erotic belly dancing. But it isn't until I arrive at the outdoor stage that the grandeur of the event strikes me. The set is backdropped by a wall roughly fifty metres long by five metres tall (the approximate dimensions of a two-storey strip mall), stuccoed to look built of white stone and crowned by copper-topped battlements.

The wall incorporates a two-storey archway, Shakespearish balconies, switchbacking staircases, wooden terraces, and various entranceways — some the width of a single doorway, one the width of a two-car garage. Doric pillars hoist up a large veranda, the jutting promontory of the second storey, which casts a long shadow across the stage's dirt, where hapless crocuses push themselves into bloom.

Stage left of the set wall grows a sprawling lawn of golf-green grass, a copse of poplars and wild sage, a functioning well, and a baptismal pond. From the pond, a stream springs forth and winds towards the audience before being gathered in a drainage ditch that's hidden by two wooden boats. Farther left is a tomb cut into the valley's side. Atop the tomb, halfway out of the canyon, three towering crosses overlook the stage in stoic judgement.

All of this exists year-round—every trapdoor, every pulley, every spike will keep company with the snow. But what is even more impressive is how the kilometre-long amphitheatre has been nestled into the Badlands' raked rock, the layering colours of red and white earth streaming across the horizon. It's so quiet and beautiful, you can't help but want to hurt it.

I get the news that, aside from playing Herod, I am to be briefly featured as Shem (Noah's eldest son) in the play's opening genealogy sequence. The Christian Bible is essentially the story of a leafy—if not slightly incestuous—family tree, one which ultimately culminates in the birth of Jesus Christ. This ancestral chart is found in two of the four Gospels (Matthew and Luke) and serves to demonstrate that the Old and New Testaments are not composed of random characters and conflicts but rather depict the single saga of God's relationship with humanity.

Over the course of seventeen insipid verses, the Gospel of Luke individually lists the seventy-four patriarchs of each generation between Christ and Adam.[4] The Gospel of Matthew—a much more streamlined Gospel—edits most of this out and names only forty-one generations. But Luke's clinical and exhaustive approach to faith sets the tone for his overall theme: that God exists in both the grandness of Creation and the tedium of footnotes.

Barrett, I discover, is not the director but co-director. His counterpart is Jessica, who is a few years younger but uses significantly less hair product. When Jessica speaks to the cast, she is constantly asking

---

4   Again, for the sake of comparison, Luke's entire scene depicting the death of Jesus lasts five verses.

everyone to settle down. Barrett, on the other hand, possesses the ability to simply *think* the cast into silence. I felt these telepathic commands earlier that morning when, chatting with a Villager, I clammed up mid-sentence and turned to see Barrett holding his clipboard, ready to begin.

At the top of Jessica's objectives is choreographing the genealogy sequence, which is to be an intricate weaving of song, dance, and stage combat. The sequence will be composed of twenty men, ranging in age from Adam, played by a teenager, to Saruch, played by a gentleman who may have witnessed the Old Testament firsthand.

Jessica calls everyone into a huddle, where she squats beneath us. "This is going to be spectacular," she says as the last men drag their heels into the group. "There's going to be a lot of ideas from you guys, but this will be a very complicated sequence, so I need you to hold those ideas until after."

Arphaxad raises his hand and, before called upon, asks, "After what?"

Jessica stutters.

"She means after the summer," Jacob says.

Jessica pitches us her vision. "It's going to be fast, it's going to flow, it's going to be"—she searches for the word—"spectacular."

She guides us through the blocking, but a couple of men stay behind, whispering in their own little circle. "And then," Jessica says, her eyes alight, "after we've built the throne of David, we then swirl the fire in a circle—more of an oval—and the music booms, and *snap* all flames are extinguished at the same second."

Noah raises his hand.

"You have a question?" Jessica says.

Noah nods.

"And you're sure it's a question?"

Noah nods.

"Not an idea?"

Noah lowers his hand.

We begin with the sequence's musical component. "And remember," the Musical Director tells us, "Jessica will have you waving your arms around like lunatics, so take in as much breath as you can."

He conducts us through the various harmonies and canons, none of which we are able to sustain. As a result, the cast spends most of our time bumming around stage, waiting for the music to cue up again.

"This is what it takes to make something spectacular," Jessica tells us, before hoofing it up the twenty-seven rows to where the sound booth is perched. While she is gone, the Stage Manager dismisses us for dinner.

"They make it too ambitious every year," King David whispers to Jacob as they walk to the parking lot.

"Get ready for the train wreck," Jacob whispers back.

⊞ ⊞ ⊞ ⊞

Every Saturday, there is a cast-wide potluck at the campsite. I am ladling some of my curried lentils (the only vegetarian dish that isn't a bag of chips) onto my plate while chatting with Simon Peter's Wife.[5] She is telling me of the time she was at the Calgary Stampede, in the box seats and watching the rodeo, when she heard the voice of God.

"And then a third time, right beside my ear. He said, 'Get to the daycare. You don't have a second to lose!' So my mother and I leave the rodeo—not even staying until the bull riding, running red light after red light. We get to the daycare and the caregiver says, 'Your son is fine, but a woman tried to pick him up.'"

Beside us, Diabolos takes a hock of ham from his slow cooker and, with two butcher knives, begins to shred his pulled pork with such zeal that hot juice splashes onto my cheek.

I turn back to Simon Peter's Wife, whose eyes are as large as shekels. "Later, my son tells me, 'I know who that woman was.' I had a

---

5   Many female characters do not have names and are only defined by their disability (example: Blind Woman) or their relationship to a patriarch. The role of a male character's wife (such as Simon Peter's Wife) should not be confused with a male actor's real-life wife.

friend from high school who was dating a Kuwaiti man, and every time I met him, he would always hold a book in front of his face."

By this point, I have lost all track of the story. The rodeo, the woman, and now international intrigue.

She says, "I told this to an RCMP officer, and he was like, 'Oh, yeah. Kuwait has a huge child sex ring.'"

"Wait," I say. "Your high school friend was a sex trafficker?"

"No," she laughs. "Was *dating* one. And, I don't mean to brag"—she leans in—"but my son was beautiful." She says it again, accentuating each syllable. "Byoo-tee-full."

I don't know the appropriate reaction for this. I want her to see that I agree with her but I also don't want her to think I am agreeing *too* much. I say, "Sounds like it."

"So the RCMP officer tells me that once the Kuwaitis have a target, they do not stop. And there's nothing anyone can do. So I put it to the Lord and said, 'Where should we go?' And He answered."

All this in response to my question, "What brought you to central Alberta?" Though, to be fair, she had asked if I was "a believer," to which I said yes. Not two days in, and I had only one lie left to spare.

⚓ ⚓ ⚓ ⚓

I'd been making small talk with him all weekend before I realized he is Judas. While the rest of us have been surviving the outdoor rehearsals of mid-May by wearing sweaters and raincoats, he's been rocking sunglasses and a leather jacket, chewing an immortal stick of gum. His bed-headed hair is slanted up and to the side, and even though it has been overcast all weekend, he has acquired a slight sunburn.

This is to be his second year as Judas. "I need people to see the humanness of my failure," he tells Pontius Pilate, who is sitting beside him in the audience. "I need them to recognize themselves in me."

Judas and Pilate are two of the rare cast members who also act outside of the Passion play. Pilate, who manages a Jiffy Lube and is a recently accredited member of Canada's actors' union, is holding the

36

cast list. "They've spelt it 'Pilot,'" he says, "like I'm flying a fucking helicopter."

I am drawn to his curse like a moth to an inferno.

"I mean," he says, "how hard is it to read the motherfucking Bible?"

We are in the sixteenth row, watching onstage for the umpteenth time as a group of Villagers open their shops. Two Carpenters chisel some spears, a Greengrocer hawks some anachronistic bananas, and the Intern Director comes across the loud speakers to tell the shoppers not enough people are visiting the basket weaver.

Pilate and Judas regard all this with the semi-detached air of high school burnouts watching football practice, their feet up on the seats in front of them. I adjust my slouch to match theirs.

‹ SCENE 4 ›

As we unwrap our snack-time granola bars, I ask Lead Drummer how he likes the Luke script compared to prior seasons. We are on our Sunday afternoon break, and the sun hovers above the amphitheatre.

"They don't whip Jesus in Luke," he says, "which is too bad because it's very pleasing." He reaches out to halt me. "Visually speaking, of course."

"Of course," I say.

More than the historical, political, or geographical discrepancies, the four Gospels differ most notably on what kind of person Jesus was. The Gospel of Matthew has the Jesus everyone loves, compassionate and charismatic. In the Gospel of John, Jesus is more philosophical, offering some of the Bible's best-known catchphrases. Mark's Jesus is the most dramatic, moving at a breakneck pace.

But the Gospel of Luke's Jesus is—how to put this?—a bit of a dick. He speaks in condescending and contradicting riddles, He's brash and impatient, and He lapses into the third person like some 1990s professional wrestler: "The Son of man cometh at an hour when ye think not." In the Gospel of John, one of Christ's most famous quotations is, "A new commandment I give unto you, That ye love one another." In the Gospel of Luke, the equivalent is, "He that is not with Me is against Me."

"Jesus is so mean," Litia said upon first reading the script. "He's not supposed to be mean."

"Well, you don't believe Jesus to be anything," I said, snatching the script back, "so maybe you shouldn't be casting stones."[6]

---

6   John 8:7. See? He's everywhere.

The Gospels also disagree when it comes to Christ's first miracle. In John, the first miracle is the crowd favourite of water into wine; in Matthew, it is healing Simon Peter's Mother-in-Law. In the Gospel of Luke, it is Jesus driving out a demon from Man with Evil Spirit, as shown in Scene 9b: Two Synagogues.[7] Herod is not privy to the miracle, so during this scene's rehearsal, I drop in on the volunteer manager, Sienna, as she turns off her computer for the day. Sienna has been involved with the CBPP for fourteen years in a variety of capacities, from acting to administration.

"It all started," she says, "when my mom shipped me off to a summer camp which she didn't know was connected to the Passion play." The story hits even closer to home when Sienna says that both her parents are atheists but the play / summer camp converted her to Christ.

I ask her what roles she has played, and she says mostly Villagers and Brides. "One year," she says, "the director didn't know how to cast me because he said it would confuse the audience if I were one of the followers of Christ, since people would wonder why Jesus didn't heal me."

Sienna's hands are half-formed. From each balled-up fist, her fingers pivot out like the devices of a Swiss Army knife.

She says, "They call it a 'congenital hand deformity.'"

"What caused it?"

"Nobody really knows. Might be genetics, might have been my position in the womb. One doctor said it was because my hands pushed through the amniotic sac and froze in their development."

I screw up my face.

"I know," she says. "But people believe some weird stuff."

Her desk phone rings. She looks at the number and ignores the call. "It's after five."

As the number of interested (let alone competent) volunteers continues to dwindle, the burden of cast recruitment has fallen on

---

7   Man with Evil Spirit also goes by the name Man once he has been healed by Jesus. Curiously, this name change is not afforded to Blind Woman or Deaf Girl who, post-miracle, are still referred to by their former disabilities.

Sienna's shoulders. For whatever reason, men do not join the play at the same rate as women. This imbalance of gender is doubly difficult because the number of male speaking roles doubles that of their female counterparts. Of course, this problem could be remedied by the age-old theatrical practice of cross-dressing.

I ask, "Do female actors always play female characters?"

Sienna says that sometimes a few Temple Guards will be women because they can wear black bandanas over their faces (for our season, Temple Guards 6 and 7 will be masked women), but this is the exception to a rule that ordains boys will be boys and girls will be girls.

"Do you wish there were more female roles available?"

She throws her head back. "All the time. It's a difficulty we run into every year because it is such a male-centric script. I know that the script committee is working towards, perhaps, a female narrator. But especially around here, these things take time."

The script committee is composed of three board representatives and a member of local clergy. And while the committee does not write the script, they sanction it.

Sienna says, "There's an importance a lot of people hold in gender. I know that even with this script, having a Holy Spirit as a female was something that people definitely had issues with."

Like most theatre companies, the CBPP is facing an aging audience. But the CBPP is also facing an aging ideology. In recent years, there have been subtle attempts to subvert traditional Christian norms while still upholding the organization's raison d'être: for people to come "from all corners of the world to experience firsthand who Jesus is." Yet among the cast, there are murmurs that a tsunami of secularization is coming: musical interludes, rimshot punchlines, a general parting of ways with the Scriptures. And each actor will have to decide whether to swim with the show or sink like martyrs, anchored to their convictions. Just recently, Barrett deleted a parable of Christ's that appears twice in the Gospel of Luke but has been deemed narratively redundant in our script. In its place will be a joke about the Apostle Thaddeus shitting himself. Cast reaction was mixed: Woman (Scene 20) was unimpressed at losing a line; Thaddeus was elated at gaining one.

"I would like to see us expand our demographic," Sienna says. "The people who come see the show are of a certain age. In the next little while, we will need a different generation. I'm thinking of the atheists."

I ask her where she would situate her idea of Christianity in relation to the rest of the cast.

"With concepts of gender, I have very different beliefs than most here. Same with homosexuality. But a lot of this is from how I grew up."

I point out that her understanding of human rights comes from an atheist background.

"I wouldn't say it's informed by atheism," she says, "but it's certainly not informed by religion." She rubs her eyes with her with her fists, and in doing so, I can tell she has lapsed into some other conversation, one she has had a thousand times before. "I'm just so tired of people being told they're going to Hell."

The phone rings again, and we wait until it quiets. "The world," Sienna says, "is full of injustice, but at the same time I need to believe that some good will come from it."

"Why do you say you *need* to believe instead of *want* to believe?"

"Because it's too hard otherwise."

I will hardly talk with Sienna after this, and when we do meet there will always be an awkwardness to our conversations, like we have revealed too much of ourselves.

The phone rings again, and she says she needs to take it. Out her window, I see that the rehearsal has finished, as has the Lord's first miracle.

As I stand to leave, I ask her, "When that director kicked you out of being a follower of Christ—who did you wind up being?"

"Herodias," she says, covering the receiver with her hand. "Your wife."

On the drive back to Calgary, I call Litia.

"Oh sure," I tell her. "They're all very nice and normal until you remember we're in the Badlands pretending to be Jews."

"Have you met Jesus?"

"No," I say. "But I think I saw Him during snack. He was wearing tight white pants and eating a cinnamon bun with a knife and fork."

Outside, the fledgling stalks of canola wave a pulsing green. Once you're out of the valley, the prairie is so flat that you can see weather systems two days away. Tomorrow night, there will be rain.

"Did you talk to anyone from Heaven?" she asks.

I tell her how, in the fading hours of Sunday's rehearsal, just before we were released for the week, the Holy Spirit sat beside me backstage. The Holy Spirit, believe it or not, goes to my old high school. "Go Rams," I said, holding my pinky and index fingers like horns against my forehead.

"Go Rams," She echoed, mirroring the gesture.

I asked Her how high school is going, and She told me that She loves dance but knows that She will have to choose between that and Her faith.

"Is it hard to choose between things You love?" I asked.

"Not if you know what you want," She said and was called back to the stage.

At my grade nine graduation, after I had taken my seat in the pews, Father Murphy read to us from the Book of Psalms: "Thou openest thy hand, thou satisfiest the desire of every living thing." And Jason D'Souza sniggered, thinking of opening his hand to satisfiest his own desires, but I felt only fear. Not just because I didn't know what I desired, but because I no longer believed there was someone who could tell me.

Herod was not the one to turn Christ's story tragic; it was the other way around. More than killing Christ, what Herod wanted was to be saved by Him. The Gospel of Luke describes the ways which

Herod, deluged each day by charlatans, pleaded to the Lord for a miracle, begging for belief, but was offered only silence. Of all the characters in the New Testament—the prostitutes, the tax collectors, the droves of nameless rubberneckers—Herod was the only one who never heard Christ speak.

There are stories of this play. Stories of strange events, stories that confound all rationale. "I have seen things," Noah told me in the lineup for Sunday brunch, "that you would not believe."

"Tell me," I said. "I can believe."

But he did not, for he knew I could not.

It seems to me that religion is for those who are strong enough to save themselves, like Sienna, like the Holy Spirit. But what if you are too weak to believe in what you cannot see, what if you are too scared to be saved, what if you are Herod?

‹ SCENE 5 ›

Two weeks into rehearsal, Diabolos and I strike up a carpool. We are both commuting from Calgary, the city I was born in and to which I recently moved back after my writing career did not begin with the meteoric success I had financially planned on.

He parks his Jetta out front and hugs me hello. In doing so, I realize that I am—quite literally—twice his height. I sit shotgun and stare at his hands on the steering wheel; his fingers are so stubby it's like they're missing the middle knuckle.

"I saw the updated cast list," I say. "Martha of Bethany's role is now open. Did she quit?"

"Something happened," he says. "She's not well and needs a lot of prayer."

"What happened?"

"It's private."

"Of course," I say. Then, as casual as Bermuda shorts in church, I ask, "What specifically should I pray for?"

Diabolos glances at me. "For her to be well."

We drive north of the city, Christian rock playing softly on the satellite radio. Summer construction has turned the highway into a maze of yellow and orange, but Diabolos swerves his way through the pylons. He grew up in the region and is pointing out all of the pioneer farmhouses, older than the province, that his family once visited. Dangling from the rearview mirror is a crown of thorns so large it constitutes a driving hazard.

He asks me my age, and when I tell him, he says. "I have putters older than you."

"I have putters taller than you," I reply.

He has a son my age, and when he mentions his name, I gasp. "I know him," I say. "We went to junior high together. We played on the same volleyball team. How's he doing?"

"I should be honest," Diabolos says, "his mother divorced me a few years ago. And he, um, he sided with her. He doesn't talk to me anymore."

On the horizon, I see another homestead, one that a century of wind has slanted to stand at an acute angle with the earth.

"It's his birthday soon," he says.

"What are you going to do?"

"Write a card," he answers, his voice starting to splinter. "Find a way to get it to him."

He then turns to me. "Do you have him on Facebook?" he asks, and I tell him that I don't have Facebook, an answer that disappoints both of us.

He coughs once, passes a minivan on a double-solid yellow, and asks if I enjoy the mass at the cathedral near my apartment.

I think of my last coveted lie, how much summer there still is to get through.

"I haven't gone to mass in a little while," I say.

"How long is a little while?"

"Oh, you know," I say, staring out the window. "Fifteen years."

We pass an overturned sedan in the ditch. The police have arrived, and a woman sits on the undercarriage of her supine bumper, sobbing.

"Every time I pass something like that," I say, "I think it's only a matter of time before it's my turn."

"It's in His hands," Diabolos responds, fingering the rearview's crown of thorns, "and His hands alone." The tires hit the rumble strips, and he retreats his hand and places it back on the wheel. Ten and two.

The genealogy sequence is not going well. The prop shop is far from finishing our torches, the ones which will hold the flames of life, so we are made to mime them. This miming may sound simple, but many of the genealogy's elderly members forget to stop holding their torches once they have passed them to following generations. Because of this forgetfulness, we have to continuously rewind our choreography to see who is holding what and why torches have multiplied like loaves of bread.

After Noah is caught double-fisting holy fire, stage management is sent to track down stand-in props, but all they can rustle up are a few scraps of wood and a plunger with strips of tinfoil attached to its flange. "It's from last year," Jacob whispers to me. "It should have been burned."

"What was it supposed to be?" I ask.

"The audience had the same question," King David says.

Jessica is reviewing her notes. She wears a backpack with a bladder of water zipped into it. "This would probably work better," she says, chewing the backpack's hose, "if we changed everything."

<hr />

Even though the cast spends every waking minute together, we know each other only through our roles. This afternoon, the Assistant Stage Manager interrupts Pilate and me to tell him that Vienna was offended that he swore in front of her.

"Who the fuck is Vienna?" Pilate says.

"Mike and Heather's daughter."

"And who the fuck are Mike and Heather?"

The Assistant Stage Manager consults her cast list, flipping through the four single-spaced pages.

"If someone wants to feel offended," Pilate says, "that's their own fucking problem. I didn't *make* them feel that way. I can't *make* anyone feel anything."

Judas mumbles, "Including your wife."

The Assistant Stage Manager gives up searching. "It doesn't matter who Vienna is. Vienna is a child who complained to me because she heard you swore."

"Shit," Pilate says. "That's my bad. I try not to swear in front of the kids."

The Assistant Stage Manager leaves, and Pilate rolls his eyes.

Since our roles are how we know each other, they are also how we know ourselves.

"As I was saying," he says to me, "I was Herod last year, and I fucking loved it. I was fucking free, on a quest to find something real in this life. Now I'm marching all the goddamn time."

ӿ ӿ ӿ ӿ ӿ

End of the day, and I am sitting beside the forty-litre water cooler and pretending to go over my lines. But what I am really doing is waiting for Jesus. He doesn't drink from the communal water (He has His own bottle) but, between each scene, He will slyly check His phone behind the cooler's bulk. I had expected the Lord to be one of the more loquacious cast members, but as rehearsals have progressed, He has remained so elusive that I've begun to worry the entire summer will pass without my come-to-Jesus moment.

On cue, the Lord approaches. He hunkers down and drags His thumb up and down His phone's screen. Finding nothing, He returns the phone to the back pocket of His fitted shorts.

He stands and polishes His blue-rimmed sunglasses with His yellow bandana before tying it around His neck. He performs this with effortless precision: He knows how to shine the lenses without leaving smudges, knows how to fold the bandana with parallel creases, knows when to flip His mop of hair to avoid tying it into the knot.

I clear my throat. "'Sup?"

Christ looks at me, then over His shoulder, then back at me. "'Sup?" He says. "Nothing is 'sup."

"You're from Vancouver, right?"

He undoes the top four buttons of His shirt to let His ascot bandana fall flat against His (shaved?) chest. "Right," He says. "Kitsilano."

"How do you like it?"

"I don't. It's hard making friends. And it must be like that for everyone, because I'm a really nice guy."

The Stage Manager beckons from centre stage. "We need Jesus at Simon Peter's house, please."

The Lord nods, pushes His sunglasses up the ridge of His nose, and jogs onto stage.

"Keep up the good work," He shouts at me over His shoulder.

I wave goodbye, with both hands.

※ ※ ※ ※

The day concludes with the rehearsal of Scene 10a: Simon Peter's House. Herod is the only one in the Galilean fishing village of Capernaum who has not been invited to Simon Peter's house, so I wander the amphitheatre alone. Way at the back of the audience, Jesus Understudy is playing "The Ground Is Hot Lava" along the benches. He balances on the backrest and then leaps across the aisle, landing wobbly on another bench before straightening his arms and knees like a gymnast selling a dismount.

I trudge up the audience and ask Jesus Understudy if he has time for an interview. He is perched on a backrest, where he uprights and thuds down onto the seat. "Why not?"

At such closeness, my stomach flops like a fish at how much he looks like the Lord—at least the ones depicted in the Sunday schools of my youth. He's got these North Atlantic eyes, bottomlessly blue, parted by an aquiline nose. A shock of tousled brown hair, a robust beard, and eyelashes thick as a giraffe's. And then, to drive it all home, he opens his mouth to reveal a fan of somewhat sallowed teeth. But it is the teeth—the humanness of them—that complete the whole look, opening the smallest door of Christ-like approachability.

I sit beside him, and we watch rehearsal. Simon Peter's Mother-in-Law lies stage left, in a bed and smouldering with sickness. Jesus, however, has arrived—stage right and righteous.

Jesus Understudy has been with the play for a decade. He has been Thief on the Left Cross, Master of the Banquet, and Judas (×2). Last year, he was finally promoted to be the real-deal Jesus but has now been demoted to backup.

There have been eleven Jesuses over the CBPP's history. There has been Old Jesus, Biker Jesus, Athletic Jesus, Fat Jesus, and Professional Model Jesus (whose real-life wife played opposite him as an Oedipal Mother Mary). But by far, the most celebrated Jesus was the Jesus of two years ago, a Jesus widely believed to be the Best Jesus Ever.

Once appointed by the directorial team, Jesus actors usually have the role until they choose to leave. When the previous Jesus (the aforementioned Best Jesus Ever) stepped down after a three-year tenure, the *Drumheller Mail* published a lengthy lament, written with the grand solemnity that comes with the end of an era, like we were once again switching from BC to AD in order to ensure that we'd never forget our tryst with perfection.

This year, however, the directors made the unorthodox move of asking Jesus Understudy to audition again. After an audition with Barrett that was reciprocally awkward and passive-aggressive, he was offered the slap-in-the-face of Understudy. He is dating the Head of Sound and didn't want to be away from her, so he decided to accept the role—a decision he is already regretting.[8] He recently found out that the new Jesus is making $1,000 more than he did as lead, cashing in at $9,000 for the summer. "When He showed up," he says, "He hadn't even been told that I was Him last year."

"Are you disappointed to not have a second go at the role?"

"I'd say so. Because in addition to being disappointed, I have to watch—" he gestures to the stage, where his better half is laying

---

8   Relationships within the cast and crew are nothing new. There have been three weddings brought about by the Passion play, and countless flings. The Passion play has also twice led to the destruction of holy matrimony, when two married actors had an affair with each other and were summarily banned from returning.

hands upon a fevered forehead. "I can be a very bitter person, but when this happened, I told myself, this isn't my horizon. I know that I'll go further. And I already have." He rests both arms on the backrest. "I'm a living statue now." For an undisclosed amount, an individual can employ Jesus Understudy to attend their party and stand so still that guests think he is an inanimate object.

The longer Jesus Understudy and I chat, the more I see an ornate sadness grow behind him. Something colourful and brittle, something like a freeze-dried bouquet: to have achieved your dream and become who you wanted to become, but then still having to live the rest of your life in the shadows of accomplishments that no longer matter.

We see Pontius Pilate—who also hasn't been invited to Simon Peter's house—walking up the aisle towards us. The audience is so large that his approach is as long as a sunrise.

For all of the Gospel of Luke's weaknesses, it does have one strength: it features women more than the other Gospels do. But there is a difference between acknowledging the equality and interiority of women and recognizing the mere existence of them, and while Luke indeed partakes in the latter, it is arguable how much he does the former. Our script—like the Gospel it is based on—divides any female character with a backstory into one of two groups: whores (Mary Magdalene) and virgins (mainly Mother Mary and the Holy Spirit, but also Martha of Bethany and two stewards of Christ named Joanna and Susanna).⁹

"It's our most feminist script yet," a member of the Angel Choir (male) told me last week, a statement I mocked ruthlessly in my notebook, until next Monday at home, when I found myself repeating it to Litia.

"Feminist?" she said.

---

9   Minor female characters can be largely clumped into one group: shrill crones. Members of this group include but are not limited to: Simon Peter's Wife, Simon Peter's Mother-in-Law, Mary Mother of James, Widow with Two Pennies, Widow of Nain, Blind Woman, Woman (Scene 20), Herbalist, Midwife 1, Midwife 2, Midwife 3, and Current Events Villager—all of whom show up in hysterics, caterwaul a couple of lines (at most), and then hush up for the rest of the play.

"Yeah," I said, thinking of our female Holy Spirit. "Well, it's complicated," I said, thinking of all the blowback that's followed.

"And what would these *feminists* think about casting a woman as Jesus?"

"I shall ask them and find out," I replied, already knowing the answer.

Pilate is out of breath when he plops into the seat beside Jesus Understudy and me. I ask them if they foresee a time where a woman is cast as Jesus.

"I think it would be wonderful," Jesus Understudy says. "I don't think it's going to happen."

Pilate agrees. "Oh, it would destroy this place in a single season."

"The Passion play," Jesus Understudy says, "is a weird little pocket in the middle of nowhere. I think it is honestly a miracle that it's lasted this long." You can tell by the emphasis with which he says the M-word that it's not hyperbole.

Pilate shields his eyes from the sun and stares down at the stage. "I would love to see a production of *Rocky Horror Picture Show* out here. I'd also love to see a production of *Jesus Christ Superstar.*" He scratches his chin. "We probably should have done that last year."

Last year was the first of the five seasons allotted to the Gospel of Luke. Much like Stalin's five-year plans, once a five-year script has been written, it cannot be discarded, no matter how unpopular: too many wheels are in motion, too many bureaucratic necks at stake. So even after the near-apocalypse of last year, our script has remained largely the same.

Throngs of sick Villagers pile into Simon Peter's house. He tries to keep them at bay until Jesus says, "Let them come."

Simon Peter's Mother-in-Law says, "Let them come."

Simon Peter says, "Come."

"You ever notice," Pilate says, "how much 'come' there is in this script?"

Jesus Understudy buries his head in his hands.

I ask if the fault of our script rests with the playwright or the Gospel of Luke.

"Both," Jesus Understudy says. "Five years for each Gospel is a nice little idea, but 'nice little ideas' kill theatre companies."

The board, however, disagrees and has doubled down on their wager that last year's flop wasn't the fault of Luke or the script, but solely of the director; they turfed him and promoted the playwright, Barrett, into the role of co-director.

But even the Church seems disenchanted with Luke. In Christian iconography, each Gospel has a symbol paired with it: Matthew is associated with an angel, signifying salvation; Mark is a lion, signifying Christ as king; John is an eagle, because of the bird's believed ability to stare straight into the sun. But Luke? Luke is a winged cow, something that is supposed to symbolize sacrifice but also bovine boredom.

"This is the problem with trilogies," Jesus Understudy says, "but it's what Vance wanted."

As the CBPP's executive director, Vance is the captain of the company. While having no say on artistic choices, the executive director steers the business side of the ship. I recently learned that last year, when Jesus Understudy was Jesus, he was dating Vance's daughter. He's not dating her anymore, and he's not the lead anymore either. "Do you see any correlation?" I ask. "I do," he says. "I'm not an idiot. We left on good terms, but sometimes I wonder. She's with the Playback Operator now."

"Hold on," Pilate says. "I thought the Playback Operator was gay."

"So did my mother," Jesus Understudy says. He then turns to me. "Knowing what I know about Vance, I don't trust him."

"He is a fundamentalist," Pilate says, "or so he claims to be. He's started a moral cleansing—his term, not mine—and is systematically removing all those opposed to him."

"What's his endgame?" I ask.

"Vance's endgame," Pilate says, "is to create a culture that has everyone doing what he says. He believes he has a God-given authority over other people. He believes the success of the Passion play is not his goal but God's."

"Passion play will survive one way or another," Jesus Understudy says. "The amount of times Vance has said, 'We're finished!' and then a week later a Hail Mary comes in from left field…" he trails off, having mixed the metaphors of two sports he's obviously never played.

Onstage, a lone clarinetist plays — a tune so mournful it wipes away all memory of the joy that was amuck just moments ago. The Musical Director waves the clarinetist into a screeching stop, and everyone takes a ten-minute break.

"Do you think it is possible," I ask Jesus Understudy, "for someone to play Jesus and not believe in God?"

"In the past, we've had understudies who are atheists. But it's like any acting piece: the words you speak will affect you." He runs a hand through his curly hair. "That's the biggest thing about acting," he says. "Believing under imaginary circumstances."

Without thinking, I say, "That's similar to faith."

"Definitely," he replies.

Jesus Understudy was twenty-six when he played Christ, seven years younger than the Bible says he should've been. He tells me of the mindset he was in when he approached the role.

"When I was twenty, I had a girlfriend and I had all of my life figured out. I was going to marry her and I was going to become a video game designer. But she cheated on me with my best friend, and all of humanity had fallen away, and I didn't actually want to become a video game designer. And I was very sad for a very long time. I made up the word *Sorrowvast*."

There is a pause so long it's like someone has dropped a line.

"At the beginning of our sixth year together," Jesus Understudy then says, "I physically abused her. I spat in her face, I picked up a chair and I threw it, she tried to leave, I grabbed her from behind with an arm around her throat."

I do the math in my head and realize he did this either right before or right after he became the Lord.

Pilate says, "Your personal experience comes with you on set. I mean, I can play a biker, but I'm not a biker. But I know how to be a piece of shit."

The three of us take a moment to watch the empty stage.

"I should add," Jesus Understudy says to me, "it's never happened since."

"Of course," I say.

"No," he says, "not of course."

The evening's birds have emerged. Chickadees. Their bodies the size of a baby's fist, but even in January or February they don't migrate away. And there's a certain respect you've got to have for something that sticks around where it obviously shouldn't.

⌐ ⌐ ⌐ ⌐ ⌐

Sunday morning, and Cleopas emerges from his RV with an old-timey bugle and trumpets the campground to Worship. The Apostle Bartholomew brought his synthesizer from home and greets us with a gentle chord progression on the piano as we hug each other good-morning. We watch the sun filter through the canopy in long spokes of light. The beams touch us, and when I look at my cast members, it seems as if their faces are what's shining, spotlights upturned into the sky.

Afterwards, I run into the Holy Spirit exiting Her tent with Her shower bag in hand. I ask what happened to Her real-life sister, Martha of Bethany.

She slides Her feet into Her flip-flops. "I'm not supposed to talk about it," She says and jogs away, each step the sound of a pin nail being shot into wood.

‹ SCENE 6 ›

The time to be Herod is at hand.

I am backstage with Nicodemus as he tells me and Joseph of Arimathea why he only has nine fingers,[10] when I am beckoned to the costume department. I ascend a stairway inside a neighbouring building and arrive at a small, sweatshoppy office. There is a cluster of sewing machines in the back, clacking away at machine gun pace. Fabric hangs from the ceiling, long spools of thread spike out from the wall, and metal trees of jewelry grow on every available surface. In the corner, by the two changing rooms, is a large drawing of a thermometer, something usually seen at fundraisers.

"What's that?" I ask a Wardrobe Assistant.

She sighs. "That is how many costumes we've fitted."

The number reads seventy-six, and the thermometer's bulb hasn't been filled.

Near the thermometer is a printout of Fra Angelico's *Annunciation*, a Renaissance fresco in which Gabriel visits the Virgin Mary. As per the tradition, Gabriel is dressed in a warm pink gown and Mary wears her trademark blue. There is a sign beneath the printout which says our own angels will also be costumed in rose gold and baby blue. The sign concludes by saying that *THIS IS THE DIRECTORS' DECISION* and is no longer open for debate or comment.

I have an inclination of what I am to look like. According to the Gospel of Luke, Jesus slanderously calls Herod a "fox," a name that is frequently interpreted as a euphemism for homosexual. As such, Herod is often portrayed as lavishly effeminate: he wears gold, eats fruit, is always sitting.

---

10   The story involves a child's curiosity, a stick of dynamite, and a serious lack of parental oversight.

The Head of Wardrobe presents my costume. She calls it a "golden-rod kandora," but it's a beige dress with short sleeves. After I shimmy into it, she cinches a wide green belt around my waist and holds up a red kimono for me to put my arms through. I am adorned with two necklaces, a pendant, and three rings: the large diamond fits my right pinky; the large emerald fits my left ring finger; but the third—some green and swirling stone—is too small for my remaining fingers.

"I'm worried that if I put it on," I say, "I'll never get it off."

She nods. "That happened to another Herod."

My crown is a thick gold band, ornamented with amber stones. The Head of Wardrobe asks me to sit and I do so, rigid, atop a stool. I close my eyes and feel the hollow weight of the world descend onto me.

The voice of the Stage Manager comes across the loud speaker. "We need King Herod onstage. Or Prince Herod, or Mr. Herod, or whatever you're called."

From the stool, I rise as royalty.

Barrett is waiting for me downstage. His hair has been gelled into small clumps, like a headful of porcupine quills. He is wearing a T-shirt that reads, *Arkansas: Literacy Ain't Everything!* Behind us, Chuza (pronounced with a *k* and said to rhyme with "Looza") is sitting on my chaise lounge and going over his lines. Historically, Chuza was my financial advisor. The script, however, has turned him into my grovelling manservant with sex-slavey connotations.

"So, Herod," Barrett says, "how do you see yourself?"

During the months between auditions and the Welcome BBQ, I extensively researched Herod Antipas. I could answer Barrett's question with domestic import figures, architectural achievements, and foreign policy decisions; I could say that I have been ruling for over thirty years, which is double the tenure of Tiberius, the current Roman emperor; I could say that I built a seaside city and established it as a centre for higher learning; I could say that I have staved off countless rebellions and uprisings, all without overreaching into massacre.

And indeed I am about to say all this, but over Barrett's shoulder I see the Intern Director instructing a horde of Dark Angels to claw at the walls of Jerusalem. "Like hungry wolves," she says. "Very good. My hungry, hungry wolves." I look behind us to where Jessica is instructing a group of Baptizees how John the Baptist will dunk them without getting water up their noses. Then, all around us, the Musical Director is leading a group of Fishermen in Hebrew song.

I twist the third ring onto my finger. "I am someone," I say, "full of religious disposition while being empty of religious belief. I am incredibly bored and incredibly sad, and I am willing to go to extreme lengths to breathe just a little bit of beauty into my life."

Barrett checks his watch. "Sure," he says. "We can start with that."

He calls action, and Chuza informs me of some shyster preaching along the banks of the Jordan River, and before I know it, I have given myself to the scene. I shiver and shake, I whisper and scream. I berate Chuza and then lift him back up. At one point, when Chuza stumbles on his line, I move to backhand him, and his fear is so genuine that I pinch his cheeks with affection. When I say the scene's concluding line, "Let's pay a little visit to the river," I roll the final *r* with such luxury that I am mildly aroused.

I storm into the audience, my long kimono snapping behind me. I am waiting for Barrett to shout "cut," but it never comes. By the tenth row, I stop. The Baptizees, the starving Fishermen, the hungry, hungry wolves — everyone has stopped to watch. All I hear is the sound of my panting.

Pilate, who has been sitting in the audience with his feet propped on the backrests, begins to clap. Alone at first, then joined by others.

It's quite startling, really, how quick a little bit of power goes to your head. Before the costume fitting, when I was wearing shorts and a T-shirt, I was the hero of the common people.

"You two are doing a great job holding those poles," I told my Bannermen backstage.

"Please," I insisted to Herod's Advisor, "let me carry my grapes."

"Your boss should appreciate you more," I whispered to Pilate's guard.

But within the course of the day, I go from the man who gives Temple Guard Captain my last bagel just so he likes me to jabbing Arphaxad in the sternum with my golden sceptre to force him to walk three paces behind me while I ascend the backstage stairs.

Onstage, the sun is heavy. My jewelry reflects sparks into my eyes while my belt pools sweat against my back. Chuza keeps interrupting my lines, and Herod Attendant 2 isn't moving the umbrella to keep my eyes in the shade. "Just follow the sun," I say. "Every planet does so quite easily."

Instead of ingratiating myself to the cast, I now spurn them. Surprisingly, this rejection turns a corner in their relationship with me: from amicability to authenticity.

"It's like they've been told their whole lives that they're unworthy," I tell Litia over the phone as I roam the hills during snack. "And they get off on it."

"That's so sad," she replies.

"Well, they've also been told that everyone else is, like, *super* unworthy—burnably so."

Backstage, Pontius Pilate and I get in a pissing match about who has more power. The Bible is clear that we hate each other but isn't clear about who answers to whom. Since we both preside over separate Roman territories, this is usually a moot point, but we meet during Scene 13: Pilot Goes to See Herod. When he enters my garden, the stage directions instruct me to bow to him, something I refuse to do.

"Emperor Tiberius doesn't even like you," I say. "He just gave you Judea after my brother went crazy and killed a bunch of people."

"That is a reoccurring theme," Pilate says, "within your shitty family."

"Who's ruled longer?"

"Who has a sword as a part of his costume?"

He is decked out in his chrome armour. His breastplate (which he insists on calling his "chestplate") makes him look chiselled, but his belly pudges out at the waist. I cross my legs to keep the breeze out of my dress.

I rifle through my backpack and emerge with a book, one with an academically austere plain cloth cover. "This is *Herod Antipas* by Harold W. Hoehner," I say, hoping to bore him into submission. I flip it open to a map. "Point to your territory."

"I know that I'm in charge of Judea and you're in charge of Galilee, but if I wanted —"

"And Perea," I say. "Galilee *and* Perea."

"—but if I wanted, I could invade you tomorrow." He says it again for emphasis. "To-fucking-morrow." Behind him, Judas and Abel snicker.

"Where are you getting this from?" I demand. "What are your sources?"

He pulls his phone out from his tunic and searches an online encyclopedia. I flip furiously through my book. I'm not looking for anything in particular, but I want to give the impression that a landslide of facts is coming his way.

"I'm in the fucking equestrian class," Pilate replies, scrolling through the article. "You goddamn have to bow to me."

Shepherd 4 saunters by, tying his cloak closed and whistling "Jesus, Lover of My Soul."

I scoff. "I'm King of the Jews."

Pilate scoffs back. "Don't you mean, Tetrarch of the Jews."

"Blow me," I say, careful to avoid my reflection in his breastplate.

We take our qualms to Barrett, who is blocking Scene 15: Calling of the Sent Ones. He is discovering that the Apostles do not know who is who. "James, son of Alphaeus!" Jesus calls, and two people stand. Next, the Lord beckons for Philip and nobody rises.

"Let's take a break," Barrett whispers to the Stage Manager, who dismisses everyone for ten minutes.

Pilate and I corner him, but he is deaf to my objections that the script has a deeply flawed understanding of first-century politics.

"He threatens me with stationing Roman soldiers in Fort Antonia," I say. "But Fort Antonia is *his* territory."

Barrett shows no emotion. "The line is," he says, "what it is."

"But—"

He holds up a hand, and the Stage Manager ushers us away.

Two weeks later, the cast is given a rewrite of several scenes. As punishment for my scrutiny of the script, I am now to bow not only when Pilate enters but when he exits as well. Forsaken by my own director, my own god.

"You know," Pilate says, flipping through the rewrite, "Luke 23:12 says that after the Crucifixion, we become friends."

I have nothing nice to say, so I say it to myself.

‹ SCENE 7 ›

Early one Saturday, Vance emerges from his executive director office in the basement of the cafeteria to stand stage right with his arms crossed. The Musical Director is leading us through our morning trills, and he clamps his conductorial hand shut as the Stage Manager whispers in his ear.

"Really?" he says, and the Stage Manager glances at Vance and nods. "Now?"

She nods again.

"Whatever," he says, and leaves to join the Fight Director, who is hanging out in the shade of the Garden of Gethsemane.

The Stage Manager tells us to sit in the audience, and as we file into our seats, we convert to our junior high school selves on our way to the principal's office: most are plaintive and quiet; Pilate is already belligerent, putting on his sunglasses and slanting his fedora forward; Andrew the Apostle is doe-eyed and red-faced; Noah is trying to convince everyone that nothing is wrong; I feel the urgent need to cry.

A handful of years ago, when the CBPP was teetering on the cliff of financial ruin (much like where it finds itself again), Vance swooped in to reverse the enterprise off the abyss of bankruptcy.

"As much as we harp on Vance," Judas told me one night in the campground, "he kind of saved this place. Before him, we had an executive director who believed that if we prayed hard enough, money would come." This business model proved nearly fatal.

Now, however, Vance is entrenched in rumour: lavish personal expense accounts, a country manor, a six-figure salary. He employs his daughter as Production Manager despite her having no experience in the role, and his sister as Social Media Coordinator despite her being middle-aged and posting bi-monthly advertisements on Twitter with floating captions that read: "Add a little bit of body text."

The Stage Manager hands Vance a microphone.

"I've heard rumours that people are upset," he says. "And we're a family, right?"

Everyone takes his question as rhetorical except Noah, who shouts, "Correct!"

Vance says, "So what do families do?"

"Argue!" shouts Noah.

"Well, yes, but they also talk things out."

"Talk it out!" shouts Noah, and Capernaum Villager 4 (his real-life wife) puts her hand on his shoulder.

"So," Vance says, "if you have anything to say, now is your time to say it."

Aside from the sound of two hundred sandals being shuffled, there is only silence. I glance around the audience and see that our massive cast takes up hardly a couple of rows; for the first time, I begin to understand how many eyes are destined to be fixed upon us.

Bartholomew raises his hand, and Vance passes him the microphone.

"Is it true that we're getting rid of 'Canadian' from our name?"

Vance retrieves the microphone. "Yes," he says, and with astonishing synchronicity, the cast inhales sharply. "As of next year, we are simply the Badlands Passion Play. We are entering a period of rebranding. The only reason we were the *Canadian* Badlands Passion Play was that there were places in the States that did something similar, but they're all bankrupt now."[11]

---

11   The rebranding also means that all of the CBPP's merchandise in the recently renovated gift shop is now being liquidated. Tomorrow at lunch, there will be a fashion show in the cafeteria, where volunteers catwalk various articles of clothing adorned with the outdated logo and being sold at clearance. "That vest only ten dollars?" Retired Shepherd says, to which Distressed Father responds, "Yes. This vest only ten dollars."

Something about their exchange strikes me as eerily familiar — the forced projection of their voices, the overlapping of answer and response, the mugging to the audience.

I turn to Judas, who is pushing french fries around his plate. "Is this," I say, "scripted?"

"Probably," he replies without looking up.

Vance is referring to the Black Hills Passion Play in South Dakota. Often regarded as North America's original Passion play, Black Hills had an auditorium that seated six thousand and was the region's second-largest tourist attraction, bested only by Mount Rushmore. In 2008, after sixty-nine years, attendance rock-bottomed and the company dropped its curtain for good. But there do remain three other large-scale Passion plays in the United States: *The Great Passion Play* in Eureka Springs, Arkansas; *The Promise* in Glen Rose, Texas; and *The Thorn* in Colorado Springs, Colorado. However, the CBPP is fundamentally different from these. Eureka Spring's production is a small part of a much larger tourist trap called the Holy Land Tour, in which visitors can watch a master potter spin a vase, take in some singalong dinner theatre, and get their photo taken with a section of the Berlin Wall. Glen Rose's *The Promise* is more similar to our play; it was conceived just a few years before us and is also staged in an outdoor amphitheatre. Like the CBPP, it features a humongous cast of human and animal actors and focuses not just on the last days of Jesus but on His entire life. Its website, too, runneth over with typos. Yet despite these similarities, there is one glaring difference: *The Promise* has caught the Andrew Lloyd Webber sickness. *The Promise* is a musical. Our own script has its flirtations with music — the genealogy dance sequence, the Angel Choir harking the new king, and Simon Peter and John the Apostle inexplicably crooning to Mary Magdalene — but *The Promise* has 150 actors high-kicking Christ's entrance into Jerusalem. Sometimes tambourines are involved. Because of *The Promise*'s genre, our cast regards it as not just subpar but subhuman, only slightly better than Colorado Springs' *The Thorn*, which utilizes martial arts and aerial acrobatics to offer a play that is half New Testament, half Cirque du Soleil.

"Thank you for your question," Vance says to Bartholomew and then points to a Villager at the far end. The microphone is bucket-brigaded towards her.

"I thought we were going to be called the Badlands Amp," she says.

More divisive than dropping "Canadian" from the name is the CBPP's new venture of renting the stage under the name the Badlands Amp to various bands and country singers in the off-season.

Vance says, "We want to get away from the stigma of the Passion play and its niche, so we are splitting our business model: our amphitheatre will now be home to the world's greatest Passion play *and* very famous musical acts." He touches the microphone to his lips. "Anyone heard of Randy Bachman?" (A smattering of applause.) "Or John Michael Montgomery?" (Significantly less applause.) "Thank you for your question."

Chuza asks whether the CBPP sees their primary venture as the Passion play or as "concerts of rock and roll."

"When we're performing the play, we are the Badlands Passion Play. But we need to cover our operating costs, so we have decided to host a select number of bands. But the crosses," he says, pointing to Golgotha, "stay up! Thank you for your question."

A Dark Angel shouts, "So do we do concerts or Passion plays?"

"The people who come to our concerts aren't like us—they ride motorcycles and drink beer."

"I drink beer," says Pilate. "And motorcycles are stupid."

Vance feigns deafness. "But our exit surveys at the concerts show that the vast majority of the audience was interested or somewhat interested in seeing our play. Thank you for your question."

Now emboldened, several other cast members raise their hands, but the Stage Manager looks at her watch and says we need to start rehearsal. Vance retreats to his underground office.

Instead of quieting the rumours, Vance's chat session has only provoked them. Backstage, as we change into costume, the whispers hiss so loudly they sound like a cloud of locusts approaching. Pilate and I lean against the sheep pen, waiting for our cue. "I was here for the first season," he says, chewing a stalk of straw, "and the way things are going I'll be here for the last."

That day, after lunch, I'm about to use the cafeteria's downstairs bathroom when Vance calls me into his office. There are washroom stalls for the actors upstairs, but the downstairs bathroom (for the administration) has painted walls and potpourri.

"Herod!" he calls from the hallway. "You have time to chat?" He turns around and enters his office, leaving the door ajar.

My hand is on the bathroom's doorknob, the five helpings of vegetarian chilli bobsledding through me. I release the handle and follow.

Vance's office looks as if a search warrant was just executed. His desk is shingled with loose-leaf, back-broken books, and orphaned electronic equipment. The shelving unit behind him sags with overflowing weight: a solved Rubik's Cube, steak knives, a fake plant now greyed with neglect. The only dustless place is the black gun safe in the corner.

He is feigning busyness when I enter—like I'm here unannounced —by clicking around on his computer screen. But his mouse doesn't have much room to move, hedged in by Magic Markers and screwdrivers, so he appears to be clicking the same spot, over and over again.

He gestures for me to take a seat. I remove the chopstick on the cushion and add it to the pile on his desk.

"I've heard Judas is quite unhappy," he says, "and I've heard he has globbed onto you."

It is true that Judas is quite unhappy, and while I wouldn't have used the verb *globbed*, it is also true that we've struck up a friendship. Last week, he drove me to O'Shea's ("The Finest Casual Dining experience in Drumheller"), where I ordered a beer and he got ice water. This is his ninth year with the play, and even though he is irritated by how this season is going, he spent the first half-hour of our conversation waxing nostalgic. He told me about the year the Passion play sheep contracted scabby mouth, a zoonotic disease that forms oozing pustules on any human appendage that comes into contact with the sick sheep, pustules that take weeks to seal, during which time the infection can leap to other people, until an epidemic is declared, and twenty years later a plaque is erected at the campground's gate in honour of the diseased: "To those who held the Lambs of God."

"If you touched the sheep," Judas said, "you were gonna get this thing. Professional actors would go, 'Then I'm not touching the sheep.' But the volunteer cast was like, 'Sure, I'll pick up the sheep, I'll grab it, I'll pretend to slit its throat, I don't care.'" Wistfully, he stared out the window and into the past. "And I think that is very indicative of this play."

But aside from the play's history of animal-borne illness, everything he told me was stuff I already knew: that the script is hamstrung by cartoonish writing; that the co-director team is a sham, and Jessica is really Barrett's assistant; that the play is dying. I tried for grade A gossip, but all he gave me was that he dated the Virgin Mary last year. When I prodded him about the controversial switch in Jesuses, he only tittered and said, "There is a *lot* of political things in there," before accepting a refill of water. The neighbouring table included Diabolos, Gabriel, the Virgin Mary, and Temple Guard Captain, and I spent most of the evening lamenting that I wasn't sitting with them.

Vance reclines deeply in his chair. "Nobody else is unhappy here," he says. "It's just a one-off." He then lets the chair catapult himself close to me. "Did he tell you anything?"

The curtness of his question catches me off guard. Is he wanting me to Judas on Judas? "I'm speaking with a lot of cast members," I reply. "Though I appreciate the heads-up."

Vance goes back to his computer, clicking that same spot. "Each year," he says, "there's always someone who wants to cause trouble. And come to think of it, it's usually Judas. Actors want him to be interesting or conflicted or whatever, but the directors just need him to be bad."

"Roles come to those who need them."

But perhaps it is also true that we come to the roles we need — taking advantage of whatever stage we have to justify our lot in life. That somehow, in our auditions, Barrett's eyes corkscrewed into our chests to peer through all obfuscation and performance, to glimpse the crystallized version of our selves, the part that we call a soul.

Take Judas: how what he once loved he loves no longer and, feeling rejected, answers with anger. Pilate, brash and bellicose, chafing at his superiors' disconnect with what is happening on the ground. Mary Magdalene is furtive and luminous; Simon Peter, bumbling and boorish. Christ Himself flounces around stage with both the wonder and the pride of the Chosen One. And then there is Diabolos, who, with a son who no longer acknowledges his existence, has hit brimstone bottom, and now has nothing but kindness for those who find themselves beside him.

And it is not only the large roles that have eclipsed their actors. The Pharisees are erudite and unapproachable, while Current Events Villager is the campground's biggest gossip. The Dark Angels have turned into a teenage gang of the dispossessed, roaming the campground all night, wreaking havoc and draining water tanks. And my advisor, the one who promoted herself from my attendant, has begun giving me unsolicited acting advice despite only being in the scene to *attend* to my fucking kimono.

Even Barrett has acquired a godlike quality — trying so hard to create something beautiful and then living in a state of perpetual disappointment with what his creation offers.

And myself? Could such closeness between how I act at home and how I act onstage really be a coincidence? The love of luxury, the flippancy that hides weakness, standing knock-kneed and limp-wristed on my balcony, staring at the philistines below and pondering how much the average person loves me. But most akin of all is the religious ambivalence so smothering it threatens to bury. Herod is a hand reaching into the darkness, where the feel of a feather touches his palm. But is it real or just another trick?

Vance says, "It might be hard for you to believe, but these characters get inside people's heads."

I say, "Really."

‹ SCENE 8 ›

June begins and so does the heat. My tent turns into a convection oven, and the hot air of the day circles within the nylon walls. I sleep outside one night, but the mosquitos get me so bad that when I wake up, my legs are leprous with bumps.

There is a hierarchy within the Passion play best understood through the assigning of accommodations: there are those within the cast and crew who stay in the on-site RVs, outfitted with desktop computers and mini-fridges, and there are those who stay in the campground, which has deteriorated into a shantytown: gaps between tents are cobwebbed with clotheslines, punctured air mattresses have been converted into tarps, tumbleweeds of abandoned towels roll along the road. This division is reminiscent of the one between French nobility and the unwashed masses, a division epitomized by Jesus.

"It is usual for a Jesus to not be super involved with the cast," Pilate told me as wardrobe assistants adjusted our costumes, "but this guy's been so distant I don't know if I could pick Him out of a fucking police lineup."

The crew doesn't grace the campground either. When I asked the On-Deck Sound Operator if he wanted to come to the campfire, he scrunched up his nose and said, "Aren't there, like, outhouses?"

Barrett and Jessica never visit. Vance does once, touring Tent City like a politician in a disaster zone, shaking hands and urging strength.

There are, of course, exceptions on both sides. Mother Mary, despite having fewer lines than me and pegging her tent mere metres from mine, finds a way to be patrician in every conversation. "What did you bring this week?" I asked her at our last potluck.

"I never bring anything," she said, rolling her eyes before slopping a heap of Diabolos' pulled pork onto her plate.

Jesus Understudy (and his cat) is an RVer, but he is so starved for the limelight that he has started visiting the campsite to perform one-man shows even though Vance has specifically asked him to stop. He mounts these illicit productions under the cloak of darkness in the far end of the baseball field to an audience so skimpy that there are hardly enough of us to spotlight him with our flashlights.

Gabriel, on the other hand, lodges in one of the coveted on-site RVs but takes time each brunch to converse with even the lowliest of No Liners. Some nights, he invites a group of us campgrounders to sit beside his RV, beneath a mosquito net in the soft shine of his summertime Christmas lights, and provides us with generous pours of high-end Scotch.

I first met Gabriel at my audition in February, which now feels like lifetimes ago—just the thought of snow seems ancient and otherworldly. He was the reader, tasked with providing the auditioning actors their cue lines. The audition was in a ballet room, and the entire northern wall was mirrored. After I read a few scenes as Herod, Barrett had me read for the role of Gabriel in Scene 4: Mary's Dream, meaning Gabriel himself (who is not fat but solid, like a Victorian strongman) earnestly read the lines of a thirteen-year-old virgin. And as I flitted about the room, pretending to be a winged messenger of God, I caught myself in the mirror. "You are highly favoured," I said to my reflection, but I didn't feel it. I am friends with other writers, real ones—writers who are publishing bestselling novels or studying at Ivy League schools or patrolling the Canadian/American border to pen cover stories on the plight of Haitian refugees. "And truly blessed among women," I told a hefty forty-year old man as I tippy-toed around in my attempt to be an angel.

One Saturday, on our lunch break, Gabriel and I venture to the Dinosaur Hotel & Bar (single rooms from fifty-five dollars a night). As I drive, he recounts for me the ideological history of the CBPP, how the invisible hand of capitalism has pushed it away from preaching to audiences and towards entertaining them.

"We used to think of the play as an evangelical method, trying to spread the story of Jesus for people in the area. But when we wrote the Matthew script, the central idea became more 'we are performing this amazing story about the life of Jesus—and hearts may be changed and the word of God may spread—but it's a *play*.' Matthew became far more theatrical, and they hired professional crew members to try and get the standard up. It was the right move."

While this move may have been economically right, many viewed it (and indeed still view it) as morally wrong, and the process has estranged many of the organization's sectarian volunteers, people whose participation is equally essential to the play's financial feasibility.

Gabriel's real-life wife is the Office Manager, and he is therefore privy to the CBPP's financial details. "When we do our concerts in August," he says, "it's a relief, because we're finally making some money to pay off our bills, and we're reaching the community in a way we never did before. It gives us a street cred that the Passion play won't. But other people find the concerts offensive."

"Like it's a secularization?" I say, pulling into the parking lot.

"Exactly."

The TrailBlazer's front end is swallowed by a parking stall's pothole. We walk across the weedy asphalt, and Gabriel pauses to root through his man purse to make sure he has his wallet. As he rummages, I stare at the marquee sign that reads *LEAM   EV YWE*. Since no English word begins with *LEAM*, the wind must have blown the spacing between the letters, meaning the options are limitless.

Lead me, every we.

Leaching men vying for wealth.

Let a meagre valley widen.

"What do you think it means?" I ask Gabriel, now beside me.

"Live music every week?"

I squint at him, disappointed. "Where is the *a* in that sentence?"

The empty tavern is dark, save for the thin triangles of sunlight that cut through the covered windows. In the corner, an oscillating fan is cranked on full but frozen to point at the lone bartender. I spot a sign directing customers to the men's bathroom but, upon closer inspection, cannot find its female equivalent.

There is a patio out back, but like everyone in the cast, Gabriel and I are being hounded by heat stroke, so we stay inside. Aside from the stools at the bar, the seating consists of wheely office chairs. Gabriel sits on one and adjusts the lower lumbar while I order us drinks at the bar.

"What do you have on tap?" I ask the bartender.

"We don't have a tap," he says.

"Then two rye and Cokes, please." I lean in and wink. "And easy on the Coke."

I carry the tumblers to the table. In Gabriel's oven-mitt hands, the straw looks so thin I'm surprised he can grasp it at all. He holds the pink plastic between his lips and takes a sip.

In addition to his role as the archangel, Gabriel is also Voice of God —a role I assumed to be important, but it's really just a three-line affair. Cuing the Voice of God's second line, Barrett's stage direction states, *a dove that looks as if it is on fire sits on JESUS' shoulder.* Unfortunately (though not unexpectedly), this special effect wasn't in the budget, and the ensuing proclamation has lost its spectacle.

The role of Gabriel, too, sounds far more significant than it actually is. Early in the script, after Jesus gets roughed up in Nazareth and escapes ninja-like through His attackers' legs, Gabriel laments:

> Oh, friends of God...
> You are the ones God has chosen.
> You are the ones God favours.
> You were made a little lower than the angels,
> And yet God has crowned *you* [emphasis in original] with glory and honour.

This is the script's only section with line breaks, written in verse like how all angels must speak. After his soliloquy, Gabriel morphs into a mute bodyguard, all but pounding his fist into his palm for the rest of the show and trying to keep his wings clean. Nothing about his storyline makes sense.

Gabriel tells me that he was Simon Peter last season but fell victim to the same cleaning-house that Jesus Understudy did. I slurp on my glass's ice cubes to tell the bartender we are ready for a refill, but he is busy wearing a bottle cap like a monocle.

Gabriel converted to Christianity in his mid-twenties. His approach to religion is much more subdued than most other actors'. Not to say he is less devout, just less la-de-da about it.

"I converted from agnosticism," he says. "Before that, the media was telling me that priests are creepy old men and that Christians are closed-minded, probably American. So when I say 'converted,' it was simply that I started reading the Bible without trying to make fun of it. I read it like I would a play, finding my role."

I slurp on my ice cubes again, but the bartender, still sporting his monocle, is now chewing on the lid of a permanent black marker as he writes something on a sheet of paper.

"I used to want to prove people wrong," Gabriel says, "so that they were left with no other option but to agree that I was right and then follow Jesus Christ." He takes another sip from his straw. "With the cast, I now deliberately duck out of conversations that start to get heated around social or religious issues, because that's not why I'm here."

He is here, in part, to make money. The cast needs to be 95 per cent volunteer for the CBPP to maintain its charitable status, and the budget for performers is divided among the remaining 5 per cent. It took some snooping, but I found out the honorariums of the paid actors. Jesus earns $9,000; Jesus Understudy, $6,000; Pilate and Simon Peter, I also discovered, are pocketing roughly $100 a week, while the Apostle James is being reimbursed $400 for gas at the end of the summer. I ask Gabriel what he makes, but he says his contract stipulates that he can't tell anyone. But he does say that, while the prominence of his role decreased drastically with the switch from Apostle to angel, his compensation has barely budged.

"I just hope they're getting their money's worth," he says. "I mean, I think the role demands a physical awareness, like puppeteering. At the beginning of the show, when Cain kills Abel, I try to show that in the wings, and the wings are an extension of myself, and I feel that takes some training." He takes another sip. "But I don't know that I would pay for this role."

The bartender walks by, sans eyewear, and stops by the jukebox to tape up his sign: *Stop kicking me!*

Not all of the Passion play's prominent characters are being compensated. Mother Mary, for example, is acting for love, not money. Ditto for Mary Magdalene. The Holy Spirit, though undoubtedly the most multi-faceted performer onstage, is paid only in applause.[12]

I voice this to Gabriel, and he says that in the history of the CBPP, there has never been a paid female actor.[13] He doesn't defend the problematic payroll but rather mentions it the way people talk about the faults of those they love, with downcast eyes and a bit of a slouch.

"But that's a systemic problem culturally," he says. "Hollywood is the same way."

Above the pool table, the light shade flickers on, casting a cone of brightness.

"This is White Male Privilege talking," he says, "but I haven't noticed any assertive sexism. Though I don't think we are actively helping the situation."

---

12 The Holy Spirit is also the only central character, including me, who has been offscript since the first week. Furthermore, She is the only central character who does not complain constantly of the heat. However, in our defence, it is a lot easier to recall your lines when twirling around in summery whites rather than sweltering beneath black robes or chrome armour or (in my case) a poly-cotton kimono.

13 Later, I mention this to Vance, and he is adamant that there was a paid female actor in the Matthew script but is unable to locate any specifics. However, he does point out that, on average, the CBPP's female staff make more than male staff because there are more female heads of departments, such as wardrobe, scenic arts, sound, and stage management.

"Us boys better watch out!" he says, elbowing me in the ribs.

Like most outlets of Christianity, Passion plays have a long repu-
tation of fostering sexism. In our play, for example, the paragon of
male sexuality would be either Pilate's sword-swinging virility or
Christ's groupie-cultivating charisma—or perhaps even me, whose
vulpine lasciviousness is a wellspring of comedic relief. Comparatively,
the paragon of female sexuality is the Virgin Mary, whose single defining characteristic is that she's never had sex.

But as bad a history as Passion plays have with fostering sexism,
they have a far worse one with fostering anti-Semitism. These accus-
ations are particularly salient when, historically speaking, the plays'
most fanatical reviewer has been one Adolf Hitler. "One sees Pontius
Pilate," Hitler declared at a 1942 German production, "a Roman racial-
ly and intellectually so superior, that he stands out like a firm, clean
rock in the middle of the whole muck and mire of Jewry." Of course,
our own Pilate stands out of our cast not so much as a firm, clean rock
than as a mound of red Jell-O, though the charge still stands: Pilate,
with his military-grade buzzcut, bristles with dignity; the rest of us
are developing dreadlocks.

And while it is impossible to make any outright link between
walking across stage with a cross and goose-stepping across Europe
with a rifle, the four-hundred-year history of the Bavarian town
of Oberammergau's Passion play demonstrates a high correlation
between who people pretend to be in costume and who they are in
their hearts. In *Oberammergau: The Troubling Story of the World's Most
Famous Passion Play*, James Shapiro writes:

> We don't have statistics on what people in Oberammergau
> believed. But we do have records of which villagers joined
> the Nazi party. And when we compare these records to
> the cast list of the 1934 Passion play, the congruence is
> extraordinary. [...] Of the leading performers, Jesus,
> played by Alois Lang, along with eight of his twelve
> apostles were members of the Nazi party. So, too, was

the Virgin Mary [...] Only Judas, played by Hans Zwink
is known to have been a "strong anti-Nazi."

Historically, we know that pogroms often erupt during the Christian Holy Week, when the scab of a two-thousand-year-old wound is ripped off and paraded through the streets. Historically, we know the Romans had far more to do with the Crucifixion of Christ than the Gospels let on. And historically, we know that not a single Jewish person has never acted in Oberammergau's Passion play nor, to anyone's knowledge, the Canadian Badlands'. That fact is doubly troubling when you consider that the play is *about* Jewish people; it's like a four-hundred-year staging of *The Vagina Monologues* having cast only white men with barbed-wire tattoos.

There's a growl of motorcycles out front, and a horde of leather jackets swaggers in. One biker repeatedly yells the term "cock meat" while another holds two empty beer bottles up to his eyes. I am the only one in here wearing glasses.

"You boys want another drink?" says the bartender.

Gabriel replies, "Not for me, thanks."

The bartender returns to the bar and free-pours a line of straight doubles for the bikers. I ask Gabriel, "Do you think anti-Semitism is always present in a Passion play?"

"Again," he says, "coming from a place of privilege and never having been hated for being a Jew, I'm not sure what the micro-aggressions are. Sure, in the play, the Jewish priests are selfish and fighting to protect their world of the Temple, but every Villager out there is presumably Jewish." The blue lights of the idling VLTs roll across his face as he stirs his ice cubes. "But during Levi's feast, I'm offstage and I see the entering priests and I hear the very Eastern music, and it's a lot of silent gesturing, and they do look like a cliché pageant of *The Jews*."

I lean in to be heard over the bikers' brouhaha. "When you ask someone backstage, 'Who are the Jews in this play?'—what do you think they say?"

"The priests in the Temple."

"Right. Or when you ask, 'What religion is Jesus?' Everyone responds, 'Christian.'"

"Really?" Gabriel says. "Oh my gosh."

"Wake up," I say. "Of course everyone onstage is *supposed* to be Jewish—but the thing that resonates is that the Sith Lords are Jewish and everyone else is Christian."

The bikers toss back their drinks, and there is a two-second swallow of silence.

"We used to bring a rabbi in," Gabriel says, "just to make sure everything we're doing was okay, but that hasn't happened for a while."

From the across the room, the bartender hollers if we want another drink. I raise my eyebrows at Gabriel, but he just smiles and shakes his head. When the bartender turns his back to us, the smile slackens from the archangel's face.

"Some of these people," he says, pressing a finger into each temple. "I see their posts on Facebook, and then see them here, and they get up and do a little prayer about loving everybody, and it is mind-boggling the hypocrisy. But, and I'm hearing my privilege more than anything, it hasn't affected me yet."

A couple of the bikers start a game of pool. The coin tray screeches closed, the table's belly *thu-thud*s open. I know they are going to be good for the fact that they don't just shove the balls randomly into the triangle but rather rack them with reason. One of the bikers takes a pool cue and leans across the table. His belly touches the bumpers, and his girth transforms into something nimble and lithe, weightless.

In school, what always struck me about angels was that they never *do* anything. Sure, they play a little trumpet and announce the odd pregnancy—sometimes they even join a baseball team. But when it comes to rolling up their robes and struggling alongside us in the muck and mire of this prejudiced world, they remain overtly absent, concerned only with keeping their feathers clean.

The theologians say they are jealous of us—that despite our not being immortal or heavenly or even winged, we manage to cultivate their contempt. But who can blame Gabriel for feeling that way, looking on as this year's Simon Peter fumbles through his lines, all the while thinking, *You are the one Barrett has chosen? You are the one Barrett favours?*

"If we're not being proactive to help women's rights," Gabriel continues, "or making a declaration against anti-Semitism, then the play's leadership needs to be better informed of what a hate crime is. But this has historically been a community where people can feel accepted and loved despite their personal failings."

I say, "But it seems the people who take advantage of that—who join this community—are only from the communities that no one else wants."

Gabriel is tongued-tied for a bit. He takes a breath. "Looking at the cast, I don't think we're at the point of just being social outcasts. We're not full of raging bigots on a crusade. But if we—I don't know how to say this—if we had people who were more progressive or liberal-minded, would it be a healthier environment? It probably would be."

The pool players continue to bend across the table, cracking the balls, which spin like planets, the pockets swallowing the colours. When the men are outside of the table's orbit, they return to being heavy, cumbersome. But beside the green, they could dance on the head of a pin.

One of the bikers limps over to the jukebox. He clunks in a couple of quarters and flips for his song. The sunlight burns through the emergency exit's uncovered window like a jaundiced eye. The men at the bar rollick at a punchline, and the Bud Light pennants that dangle from the ceiling sway in the fan's tunnel of breeze. And then the electric guitar emerges, distorted and fuzzed, followed by a snare that marches into the first verse.

When I die and they lay me to rest
Gonna go to the place that's the best
When I lay me down to die
Goin' up to the spirit in the sky

The biker turns to the pool table, his back facing the jukebox and — for no discernible reason — horse-kicks the machine.

One morning in the campground, Mary of Bethany (sister to Martha) calls me over to her tent trailer and breaks off a heel of freshly baked bread, slathering it with salted butter. She presses the plunger on her French press and pours black-brown coffee into a mug.

"Here," she says, handing me both the bread and mug.

She saw me eating a wrinkly apple for breakfast and said, "I won't accept this."

We eat together at her picnic table, and I ask her if she knows who Martha of Bethany is.

"Of course," she says. "Martha of Bethany was the sister of Lazarus. She was also—"

"I mean do you know who the new Martha of Bethany is."

"Oh," she says. "Her." She nods towards a woman in her early twenties leaning against the food truck and chatting with her real-life brother, a Roman Soldier, while she braids something with her hands. Up until this point, she had merely been Female Dancer 3. I turn back to Mary of Bethany. "Do you know what happened to the old Martha?"

Mary of Bethany brushes the crumbs off the picnic table and looks into my mug, still with a quarter-cup left. "Are you done?"

I am about to say no, but a No Liner sits beside me and starts listing the names of his thirteen cats. "Garfield, Teepee, Storm, Pickles, Doobie, Missy, Moonshadow, Baby Girl…"

Mary of Bethany takes my mug and disappears into her trailer.

"Flash, Taz, Logan, Cally, and…and…" I stand to leave. "And… and…" He palms his forehead. "And Xena Warrior," he says. "How could I forget *her*?"

"And that's just the cats," he calls to my back, "not the dogs!"

A central part of the Canadian Badlands Passion Play is the grandeur of its animal cast. Past animal actors include a rooster who could never cock-a-doodle-doo on cue, an amorous dove who found a deep and carnal desire for its reflection in a Temple Guard's helmet, and a donkey who routinely bucked off the Messiah at the sight of water.

This year's Jesus has been assured that He will enter Jerusalem on the back of a more pliant beast of burden. Our season also boasts the usual flock of white and black sheep, which have been brokered by Shepherd 3, a real-life sheep herder. Most impressively, in Scene 26a: Pilot Enters Jerusalem for Passover, Pilate now leads his battalion atop a fifteen-hand stallion named Bram. However, the magnificence of this entry is quickly dampened by the fact that Pilate has never ridden a horse, and after a rehearsal during which Bram turned skittish and nearly killed us all, the directorial team and John the Apostle (a real-life cowboy) decide that Pilate's horse will now be led by Shepherd 3 in disguise as Roman Soldier. Shepherd 3 will hold a rope secured to the horse's harness, and Pilate's reins will rest slack—attached only to imagination.

"It looks like a fucking pony ride," Pilate told me backstage, punting a Villager's thermos to send a spiral of water through the air.

After lunch, as we are filing out of the cafeteria in a conga line to slather sunscreen on the back of each others' necks, the Production Manager pulls me aside. "Barrett wants you to be more eccentric," she says. "Zany."

"I could kiss Chuza," I say.

She says, "I don't think he'd like that."

"Chuza?"

"No, Barrett."

I shrug. "I'll just improv it and see what happens."

"He was thinking more along the lines of giving you an animal."

When my own dog, Maisy, is cast as Herod's pet, I am forced to admit that the tetrarch's life has fully overlapped my own.

Litia and I adopted Maisy five years ago from the Fredericton SPCA. I didn't want a dog. Litia wanted a dog. And I wanted Litia. But half a decade of typing all day with someone curled overtop your feet has a way of welding two souls together.

Maisy will be featured in a single scene, Scene 13: Pilot Goes to See Herod, but will remain backstage throughout the rest of the show. "We're a bit short on cash," the Production Manager tells me, guiding us backstage to Maisy's kennel, "so we had to repurpose something from last year."

Stored beside the sheep pen is last season's tomb of Christ, about the size of a standard horse trailer. (This year, we are using the original tomb, which is hacked into the cliffside.) The outside has been plastered to look like stone, but inside, the particleboard and two-by-fours remain exposed.

All actors change backstage, with neither comfort nor shame. The Romans are afforded a small armoury where they can get into uniform, but Roman Soldier 5 ate a tuna sandwich in there ten days ago and the smell will not leave, so the entire legion now strips alongside the commoners. Jesus alone is provided with an enclosed backstage dressing room / shower to wash off the blood between burial and Resurrection. The tomb — my new dressing room — is several times the size of Christ's.

I look at Maisy, who is licking a bit of last season's gore off the floor. The blood is actually chocolate syrup, so I tell her to stop. She peers up at me, her soft brown irises, open and unblinking, slowly going cross-eyed at the bead of holy blood that twinkles on her nose before her tongue curls onto it.

The tomb was originally closed with a large circular stone, so there is no door. As we speak, a scenic arts crewman begins to drill a wooden gate across the entrance.

"Will she be okay in here?" the Production Manager asks, checking her clipboard.

I run my hand over the gate's rough wood. "Can we get a dressing room star on this?"

While Maisy chases ground squirrels around the baptismal pond, Barrett explains to me the blocking. I am to enter with my entourage and the dog trotting alongside. We will be playing a game of bocce ball. Two of my guests throw and land quite close to the target. I throw and land significantly farther away. Maisy sees my displeasure, runs to my ball, and nudges it closer to the target. Pilate then enters, yells at me, and departs. I demand Chuza give me a sponge bath, after which I exit offstage and Maisy scampers behind.

"Is this possible?" Barrett asks.

I look at the rows upon rows of empty seats, waiting to be filled by wide eyes, all of them fixed on Maisy. And I know that this blocking has no hope in Hell of happening. But I know she will love it here, will love swimming in the river, playing capture-the-flag in the woods, eating golden-brown marshmallows, and howling at the full moon.

"Totally," I tell Barrett, and then without fully meaning to, I quote Scene 3's Holy Spirit: "Nothing is impossible with God."

The next morning at brunch, Pilate is informed about the addition of Maisy to our scene. He is already being upstaged by a horse, and now a dog.

"Why don't we just get it over with and have a fucking panda play Christ?"

⚓ ⚓ ⚓ ⚓

At the end of rehearsal, I offer Roman Servant 1 a ride back to the campsite. I want to change into a fresh T-shirt before heading to O'Shea's, where Judas has invited me to join Pilate and Abel for a drink. Roman Servant 1 usually catches a ride with the Apostle John, but he is in another meeting about Pilate's grave horsemanship. Dusk is upon us, but the day's heat persists, and as I squeeze between two trucks in the parking lot, my bare arm is burned by the metal.

I start the engine, and we both roll down our windows. "Have you figured your character's backstory yet?"

Roman Servant 1 is the only unmasked woman cast in a male role. "I've been doing some reading on Tiberius," she replies, holding up a library hardcover on the Roman emperor, "but I'm still contemplating my personal history."

I am impressed by her research. Aside from Pontius Pilate's bullshit website, the extent of most actors' research is limited to the Gospels.

"Tell me about Tiberius."

"He was terrible," she says.

"Why?" I ask, assuming the answer will be "because he killed Christ."

"Because he fostered corruption among the governing classes of Rome," she says. "Also, because he killed Christ."

We round the highway's bend, and the river oxbows before us. The current is sluggish in the heat, and the setting sun glows the water with tiger stripes of orange and shadow.

"What's it like being one of the only cross-cast women?"

"It's a real honour," she says, "that Barrett has so much faith in my acting ability."

I ask if she is going to play her character as a man or as a woman.

"I haven't decided yet, but I think I'm going to go male."

I take my eyes off the road to look at her. "Like Mulan?"

She extends her hand out the window and palm-surfs the wind. "Just like Mulan."

A murmur of sparrows shape-shifts in an overhead current, and in the farmstead alongside the secondary highway, two American Paint Horses are running the length of the barbed wire.

"Are you a believer?" she asks.

I stall for time. "In?"

She turns her whole body to face me. "In Jesus Christ."

"Like, do I believe that Jesus Christ existed as a historical figure?"

Roman Servant 1 does not answer. She reclines her head on the headrest and closes her eyes. She is affording me mercy.

"I believe," I say, "that Jesus, at one time or another, existed. But I don't believe in the Resurrection—which, I suppose, is kind of key."

Eyes shut, she says, "That's cool you haven't made up your mind. Most people are either so sure that they do believe or so sure that they don't."

It will be the only time all summer I am called cool.

"You can't tell anyone," I say.

She opens one eye. "Would never dream of it."

When we get back to the campsite, Simon Peter is in his circle of Apostles. He calls me over. "You know," he says, wrapping his arm around my shoulder as his entourage giggles, "we have a name for you when you're not around."

He smells of sweat and Earl Grey.

"Prince John!" he says, and his entourage buckles in laughter. "You know? Like in Disney's *Robin Hood*!"

I have never seen Disney's *Robin Hood*, but I do see Roman Servant 1, who was making her way to the Apostles, stop in her tracks at the joke before U-turning towards a group of Dark Angels playing a board game about trains.

I duck out of Simon Peter's hold and excuse myself. "I'm going out," I say, "with friends."

On my way to the tent, I'm kicking the heads off dandelions. "Prince John?" I say. "Oh, you mean the man who led an empire while his brother was off losing the crusades? The man with his own Shakespeare play? The man who wrote the Magna fucking Carta? That Prince John?"

In O'Shea's, Abel, Judas, Pilate, and I take a corner booth. The rosewood darkens the room, and moonlight strains through a stained glass window of a unicorn. Flatscreens overlook the bar, each one tuned to the same sports channel. One of the former Passion play actors is featured in a commercial, and our conversation is interrupted whenever this ad comes on because Pilate punches the table and curses the actor's name.

Judas and Abel have each ordered a burger and water. Pilate has ordered a double gin and tonic and a Cobb salad since he is trying to squeeze into his armour. I have ordered a beer, the bottle's label peeled off and curling on the tabletop.

"That genealogy sequence is a fucking death march," Pilate says. "The audience is gonna shit themselves out of boredom."

In response to the genealogy ensemble's inability to remember our choreography, our dance sequence has become less an artistic exploration of the ordinance of God demonstrated throughout human history and more of an exploration of two-dimensional shapes. What was once an elaborate montage of interpretive dance has become six minutes of twenty-two men shuffling in and out of various triangles, semi-circles, and rectangles. Our choreography is now reminiscent of a North Korean military parade, yet with neither the precision nor the fervour.

Our singing has been cut as well, replaced with a recording that plays over the loudspeaker. All we have to do is say our names in two beats of 4/4 time while continuing our assembly of shapes. But this simple instruction is complicated by the fact that most Biblical names are multi-syllabic: Zerubbabel and Methuselah, Maleleel and Arphaxad.

Abel, who is only in the first forty-five seconds of the sequence before being murdered by his brother and forgotten for the entirety of the show, points a finger at Pilate. "If they cut any more of my stage time, I'll be the one to kill somebody."

But Pilate waves him off. "At least you don't have to deal with a fucking red curtain following you around like some shitty ghost."

Since Pilate's and my scenes often come one right after the other, the design department has recently crafted and debuted what is known as the Wall. The Wall is a long strip of heavy cloth approximately 1.5 metres tall by 4 metres wide and is held up by teenage Bannermen. When Pilate is onstage, the Wall shows Roman red (except it's more of a metallic scarlet); when Pilate exits and I enter, the Bannermen rotate the Wall counterclockwise for it to show what is presumedly my palatial wallpaper: several different shades of gold adorned with burgundy tassels as large as a child's severed arm.

Pilate and I hate the Wall. In fact, we loathe the Wall so much that we have bonded over it. Not only does it look like, to quote Pilate, "A heap of human shit," but the most spectacular part about the play is the set itself, and to obscure it with a cheap bolt of fabric reverses the gravitas of our scenes, giving them a distinct sideshow quality, something unpacked from a caravan and performed at a state fair for the local farmers and ne'er-do-wells. Furthermore, the Bannermen—who are home-schooled—have not built up the muscle mass that unrelenting bullying encourages, so each time there is a gust of wind, the Bannermen's bird-boned arms prove no match for Mother Nature, forcing me to flee my palace mid-scene as I sense the walls literally closing in.

The waitress delivers our food, including Pilate's Cobb salad. He scoops up the chicken and bacon and shovels it into his mouth. Mid-chew, he asks Judas how he and the Virgin Mary are doing since their breakup.

Judas stirs his ice water. "We're being polite and not really talking. It doesn't help that she's one of Barrett's students and worships him."

Barrett teaches theatre at a private Christian university in Calgary the rest of the year. According to Judas, who is currently studying at the same university to become a youth minister, Barrett has acquired a small but fervent following within the department, a following that affords him a papal infallibility.

"I'm trying to be human," Judas says, "but Barrett wants me to be a cartoon. And no matter how many times I tell him that my line 'My name is Judas, son of Iscariot' is wrong because Iscariot is where I'm from and not who my dad is, all he says is"—he adopts a computer monotone—"the line is what it is."

"At least you have lines," Abel says.

Judas grinds the heels of his hands into his eyes. "My dad's name is Simon."

The commercial comes back on, and Pilate calls the actor a "dick snatcher" and feigns throwing his fedora at the TV. The waitress behind the bar ducks and then rises tentatively. She laughs nervously, which makes all of us laugh awkwardly, and I exploit the lapse of conversation. "What happened to the old Martha of Bethany?"

For a while, it seems like the squeaking of silverware will be my answer.

Abel says his real-life wife is friends with the old Martha of Bethany, so he knows but won't say.

Pontius Pilate says he knows too, but talking about it will just get him upset.

Judas stares at his ice water.

"These goddamn directors," Pilate says, "and their drive to destroy this entire fucking community."

Abel says, "But she did something like this before, in a shopping mall."

"Sure," says Pilate. "And if she did this in any other play, it would make sense to toss her. But not fucking here."

"But what would we do if she did that during a show?"

"We would fucking work with it," Pilate says. "To see Barrett turn his back on her hurts me so much. When I first arrived at the Passion play, I was a loud, rambunctious, outspoken ten-year-old, and the directorial team had a hard time reining me in. But rather than kicking me out, they wrote in a role that utilized what I was bringing. And that is why, to this day, the script includes Demon Possessed Boy."

I glance at Judas, whose face has welled with such redness that I think him about to cry.

The waitress comes by and says they're doing last call. "But you boys don't really drink."

"Oh, I drink," Pilate assures her, "but not with these pansies."

Then, for good measure, he orders another double gin.

Abel, who is currently applying for admission into Calgary's police academy, asks, "Aren't you driving?"

"Fuck you," Pilate responds.

The commercial comes back on, and Pilate—revolted—shoves his Cobb salad into the middle of the table, the meat all gone, the lettuce never touched.

* * * *

When I was halfway through junior high, my mother took a course on flower extracts alleged to homeopathically treat "ailments of the mind." By this point, I had been to therapy, yoga, and anger management seminars led by a shrill little man with the truly Dickensian name Dr. Ricketts. Nothing had changed.

At the completion of the course, my mother received a large tool box filled with vials of flower extracts—holly, clematis, Star of Bethlehem—which she would uncork and mix into a tincture I was to drink thrice a day. "Have you taken your flowers?" she would ask each evening as she arrived home from work, regardless of whether I had a friend over.

"It's what she calls weeding," I'd explain after she left.

I don't know if the flowers worked. The internet insists they're all placebos. But I do know that the times I saw my mother not necessarily the most happy but the most hopeful was when she was perched over that tool box, dragging her finger along the lines of her textbook and comparing what she read with the notes she'd taken—moments earlier—when I had been forced to talk about my feelings for fifteen minutes straight. She'd then peruse the glass bottles, selecting one to hold up to the light, and whisper, "I found you."

This week, before I left for Drumheller, she stopped by the apartment. "I get worried," she said, handing me a self-help audio book. "This is from the library." I looked at the CD and tossed it onto the couch. "But be quick," she said. "There's a waiting list, so we'll never be able to renew."

As I was closing the door, she put her boot against the jamb. "Also," she said, "are you taking your flowers?"

Diabolos was unable to carpool, so I drove myself. During the drive back home, having surfed my way through FM radio for over an hour, I cave and slide the disc into the stereo.

Overtop a soundtrack of bells, chimes, and what is possibly a theremin, an androgynous voice emerges. *Welcome*, the voice says. *We are so glad you could join us.*

"Who is we?" I ask the stereo.

The voice is engineered with a reverb to sound as if it's calling you from the mother ship. *You will not only feel recovery but a steady maintaining will ensue.*

"What does that even mean?"

Your physical body will respond quickly to the absence of resistance.

"What the hell is she listening to?"

With every day that passes, your adjustment with well-being will become stronger, and your cells will realign.

"Jesus Christ," I say, hitting the eject button. "She thinks I have fucking cancer."

But the CD does not eject. *There is great love here for you*, the voice says, and the honesty of that phrase, its unabashed affection, catches me off guard. And my face burns so hot that I have to pull over to stand in the middle of a canola field, beneath the mist of an industrial sprinkler, as the world blooms radioactive all around me.

‹ SCENE 10 ›

For the first time in a decade, the painted lady butterfly is migrating through southern Alberta, north from central Mexico. In the campground, the butterflies rest on picnic tables and fenceposts, the ledge of the dumpster and the wooden handle of the outhouse, their salmon-pink wings pulsing like an idea trying to take form.

I had assumed that there is a point in every caterpillar's life when it begins to feel butterfly wings cutting through its skin, and it knows that the time to transform has arrived. But recently, I read that a caterpillar in the cocoon does not transform but digests itself, melting into a pile of mush the consistency of river mud. This mush is what congeals into a butterfly. Coincidentally, that process is the theme of most songs we sing at the campground's Sunday Worship, songs about impure desire and intrinsic weakness, how we must devour our shrivelled souls before we are allowed to be beautiful.

How much faith should we put in the next life? The seventeenth-century French philosopher Pascal argued for the belief in God based on a theory of probability. There is no way to conclusively know if God exists while you are alive. If He does not exist but you have believed in Him, the only harm comes from having wasted a few Sundays, acted morally superior at every Christmas dinner, and spent a summer prancing around the Badlands in a burlap sack.

But if God does exist, He will either reward your faith with infinite happiness or, if you were an unbeliever, tell you to get ready for the pain. Therefore, Pascal argued, the prudent choice is to believe in God. And for those who find themselves unable to have faith, Pascal said they should just go along with it until they forget what they pretend to believe and what they actually believe, until the script becomes so second-nature that you are no longer reciting the words but truly saying them.

Sunday morning, and Cleopas emerges from his RV and bugles us to Worship, where Bartholomew is already waiting by his synthesizer. He tells us to open our Duo-Tang of songs to page 34, and it dawns on me that Pascal's wager overlooks a critical scenario: What if the question isn't whether God exists, but rather *which* God exists?

There's really no intelligent way to say this, but up until that moment, as I watch the butterflies flit like marionettes throughout our lawn chairs, it has never occurred to me that some religions—the overwhelming majority of them, in fact—are wrong. And not just in the sense of minor dogmatic differences (differences that even the Gospels have between them) but rather completely, utterly, inconsolably wrong. With every song that Bartholomew plays for us, its final verse explaining the various ways the righteous will march into Heaven, we are also singing about the one billion Hindus who will arrive to see God and say, "Wait—aren't you supposed to be a dancing elephant with six legs?"

And of course the inverse is also true: our campground congregation is ignoring the distinct possibility that we will be given our last rites, die, and wake up as seagulls, saying, "Wait—wasn't I supposed to meet an old white guy with an intense interest in Middle Eastern politics?"

What if we dissolve ourselves in darkness and emerge merely a moth? Or what if we discover too late that we never were a caterpillar, only a worm that had wriggled its way into some stray thread and starved to death, thinking itself saved?

Suddenly, Pascal's wager doesn't seem like an insider's bet but the folly of believing you've deduced the next number on a roulette wheel. As Bartholomew plays another hymn's opening loop, the act of adopting any religion appears to me as the ultimate expression of arrogance, that you're confident enough not only to place a bet but to tell others what number they should choose, threatening them with an eternity of third-degree burns if they opt otherwise.

I don't know why it took me so long to realize this. Perhaps because doing so concludes that believing in God is the longest of long shots. And when you're gambling with how you spend your entire summer, wasting so many months seems sacrilegious.

When I take tally of my greatest fears, right at the top is not having enough time: not having enough time to read what I want to read, to write what I want to write, that somewhere in the churning future is a version of me who has died without seeing Sacramento—not that I have any explicit need to see Sacramento, but what a shame to have died not knowing what it looks like.

In the campground, I feel angry and alone. But then, as Bartholomew leads us back into the chorus and the cast sings softly about inescapable judgement, a single butterfly lands on my T-shirt, its pink vivid against the black. And is it really a coincidence that its whisper-thin body has travelled four thousand kilometres, over the Sonoran Desert's sky-scraping cacti, the Navajo Nation's immense mesas, and the ineffable boredom of Salt Lake City, weaving through thunderstorms and traffic jams, all to land at this precise moment exactly where my heart would be if I were just a smidge shorter?

⚒ ⚒ ⚒ ⚒

The genealogy sequence has become a case study in Murphy's Law. Jessica was just informed that there aren't enough lapel mics for all of us, meaning some actors will be forced to say their names without amplification.

"Can't we just project?" I ask Jacob.

"The amphitheatre is too big," he says. "We had to do that last year, and—trust me—the audience was not impressed."

Part of last year's perfect storm was an aging sound system that crapped out randomly, plunging crucial scenes into pantomime. This year, Vance has successfully fundraised for a new, state-of-the-art system, with onstage speakers camouflaged as rocks, foliage, and Temple pillars—speakers upon which, at even the slightest sprinkle of rain, swarms of sound technicians descend to throw tarps, plastic bags, and even themselves.

Jessica devises a workaround. The genealogy men onstage who do not have lapel mics are paired with genealogy men offstage who will share a hand-held microphone to voice-over their partners' names. In theory, the workaround is ingenious. In reality, it adds yet another layer of complexity. Not only must we re-choreograph to allow for the proper number of onstage versus offstage actors, but we now have to contend with teaching elderly men how to use electrical equipment.

Jessica then gets word that the budget is too tight for the sequence's final torch to be made, so she must confiscate Jacob's. This small change not only puts Jacob in a pissy mood for the rest of the day but has a chain reaction within the blocking that will need to be addressed next rehearsal.

Backstage, Maleleel says, "It could be going worse," and someone— I'm not sure who—says the same thing back in a high-pitched voice.

That night, at the moonlit campground, Judas, Pontius Pilate, and I decide to get drunk. In Judas' fifth-wheel, we chug through a six-pack before moving on to a bottle of Baileys that has been curdling in my tent for the past two weeks.

Judas slides a couple of mugs across the fold-down table. His hands are cracked with sunburn, and Pilate's wraparound sunglasses have given him a tan line so prominent it looks like he's wearing a masquerade mask.

Having now taken in the full scope of the play, the two actors are incensed by what they see as the script's secular tendencies: the showboaty Jesus, the stylized voice-overs, the still inexplicable presence of Gabriel.

"This script," Pilate says, "and its bullshit philosophical question of does God give a shit. The Gospels answers that question very clearly. John 3:16."[14]

"It's almost like our writer didn't research a goddamn thing," Judas says, glugging the Baileys into our mugs.

Pilate feigns shock and horse-flaps his lips. I take a sip of Baileys and wonder if the heat has turned the drink thicker, viscous even.

"I don't give a shit at this point," Judas continues. "Barrett's an asshole."

Pilate leans towards my recording phone. "On the record!"

"You better put that in your book," Judas says. "That can be the title: *Barrett = Asshole*."

I am taken aback by their anger, their adamance about staying faithful to the Scriptures. "But isn't a conservative ideology what's harming the Passion play," I say, "in that its audience is dying out?"

"Sure," Pilate says, "the play has an appeal to conservative Christians who have pockets that are very deep. But they need the Passion play as much as anyone else. And when they come and see it, my hope is that they will open their hearts to...to..."

Judas finds the end of his sentence: "To a broader view."

"A couple of years ago," Pilate adds, his voice buoyant with pride, "we had a homo-erotic actor as our Jesus."

"I don't know if you can count that," Judas says, "because the play wasn't really aware of it at the time."

"Well, I was aware of it, and I was there."

"And he was never Jesus again."

"Yes, it was a single year," Pilate says. "But we've also had a Villager be a transgender woman."

"Man," Judas says.

"A broader view?" I say. "Have you asked people what they think about casting a woman as Jesus?"

---

14   John 3:16: For God so loved the world, that He gave his only begotten Son, that whosoever believeth in Him should not perish, but have everlasting life.

"Jesus is a historical figure," Judas says. "I have no problem with it theologically, but we are telling a historical story."

Pilate concurs. "Lady Jesus would be the end of us. We could not recover from that."

I have heard this argument about the historical need for a male Jesus so many times that I spent the last carpool with Diabolos circling all of the script's historical reshaping that the cast is fine with: the geopolitical inconsistencies; the biographical incongruities; the omission of Jesus' entire monologue about the hellfire awaiting those who end a marriage, lest any divorcés are in the audience.

"What are you doing?" Diabolos asked.

"Just some line work," I said, closing the script, and the two of us then gazed at the abandoned homesteads, remarking on the disintegrating beauty of each one.

In the trailer, I point out these revisions to Pilate and Judas. "Our script," I say, "is fine with bending geography, politics, and even time, but the one thing it won't bend is gender."

"The problem we run into," Judas says, "is when the Bible was written, everyone was fucking sexist. But most of our cast is still of the opinion that there is nothing wrong with this Book and there are no contradictions in it."

Perhaps it is because of the long day or perhaps it is because of the alcohol, but nothing about this conversation makes sense. I don't even know if we are agreeing or disagreeing. Pilate and Judas are two of the most politically progressive members here. And yet they are also two of the foremost objectors to the script's ecclesiastical revisions, even though the text they object to manipulating has already been—by their own admission—highly manipulated.

At the start of this millennium, Statistics Canada showed that the youngest demographic is nearly four times likelier to be "Non-Religious" than its eldest counterpart.[15] If the Passion play wishes to

---

15   This disparity jumps even more when you include an adherence to "Other Religions," among which StatsCan counts Satanism.

seduce a younger audience, that means a non-Christian audience—an audience composed primarily of, as Judas puts it, "fucking hipsters."

"Goddamn Vancouver hipsters," Pilate says. "You can put that on the record."

I snort with laughter, and Judas chimes in. "Wear some jeans that fit, you retard."

"Wash some clothes," Pilate says, and the two of them get rolling.

"It doesn't have to all be flannel."

"Shave your goddamn beard."

"Suspenders aren't in style anymore."

"We should charge them triple."

"Wait," I say. "Don't you think our Jesus is a hipster?"

Judas frowns. "Little bit."

But Pilate does not think an aging demographic is behind the Passion play's woes. "Certain people," he says, raising an eyebrow in the honoured tradition of those who know they are being recorded, "like to spend money like their fucking pockets are on fire. And last year shit the bed. Like, fucking fisted it deep. Elbow, shoulder deep."

"We keep spending money on balconies," Judas says, referencing the set's annual facelift. "And why did we need new boats?"

Pilate points emphatically at his friend and knocks over his empty mug.

Outside comes a shriek of curfew-breaking Dark Angels, home-schoolers parched for teenage interaction.

"But I can see Vance's logic," I say. "Sure, we change the Gospel every five years, but the play is always the same. We need to do something that will attract audiences, because tickets aren't cheap."[16]

Judas shrugs. "People want a spectacle."

"And we're then in a position where we have to spend enormous amounts of money to change the set because we're not changing

---

16   Front row: Adult, $71; Senior, $61; Youth, $51.
      Prices include all applicable taxes. Online tickets subject to a $4 service fee. Rush tickets subject to a $5 service fee. All sales final.

anything else." I pause for a rebuttal. "I guess I don't have a question. I thought you would disagree."

"We agree," Pilate says, eyes down.

"But if that's the case," I say, "our days are numbered."

The two of them nod. After a moment, Pilate says, "My father hasn't seen this show in years because he hates this fucking artistic shit."

So the play is, like all attempts at art, a contradiction of itself, an external manifestation of an internal struggle. The division is not between the play's liberals and conservatives but rather within the heart of each individual actor, who is both liberal and conservative, unsure of how to hold on to what he loves without choking it entirely.

Over the past few days, alumni of the past shows have sat in on rehearsals. Judas has spoken with many of them. "I've heard," he says, "that the audience finds Gabriel's wingspan laughable."

"The audience can suck a dick," Pilate says.

The enormity of the failure that looms only three weeks away gathers upon our shoulders. When I stand, the room wobbles. Pilate and I lumber out of the trailer into a night that has grown damp. The vinyl siding of John the Baptist's trailer is dewy against my palm as I piss into his wheel well. I've never felt more tired.

Dark Angels rustle in the bushes. Someone has lit a match, and sulphur prowls through the air. From over my shoulder, I watch the red eyes of Pilate's tail lights disappear behind a plume of dust.

‹ SCENE 11 ›

The CBPP was born from a combination of hope and despair. During the height of the Vietnam War, a schoolteacher named LaVerne left Calgary to live in the reclusive hamlet of Rosebud (population 87), sixty minutes east of Calgary.

LaVerne is now seventy-five, a bit buck-toothed, and small birds gather around him like he is Snow White with laundry to hang. "Are you familiar with flower power?" he asks me as we sit in the shade of his paradisal backyard and drink homemade limeade. "That was why I left the city and moved here."

At the same time he did so, Drumheller's economy was in free fall.

"In 1953, fifty thousand people were living in the valley. But then the mines collapsed, and the town has never recovered. So I approached the mayor with an idea." After nearly three decades of bureaucracy and soliciting land donations, the CBPP staged its first production. But now, as he repeatedly reminds me, LaVerne has nothing to do with the play.

"I was retired," he says, "but I took a seat on the board. Vance came in, and soon after, our accountant quit because he didn't want to be associated with what was happening. So then I—oh, look!"

A wren has sat atop a nearby birdhouse, a limp worm dangling from its mouth.

"What a marvel," LaVerne says.

The grotto of his backyard has a small pond in which his granddaughter's goslings paddle around. The gazebo smells of cedar, and the firepit is teepeed with wood. When the wren takes flight, I have no idea why it would ever want to leave.

LaVerne says he quit soon after the accountant. "I couldn't control Vance," he says, "but I still get angry calls about him from donors."

"What do they say?" I ask.

"They call him New Age."

When LaVerne was the executive director, he was making a part-time salary (roughly $2,000 per month) that he donated back to the organization; he also established an investment fund to ensure the play's long-term stability. According to LaVerne, neither of these traditions has been upheld by Vance. Because of Vance's failed venture into filming the play for audiences to view in movie theatres, in addition to a Klondiker mentality that drives him to purchase as much land as possible, the investments have been looted and the organization thrust into a series of financial disasters. But, according to Pilate, while the CBPP swerves from crisis to crisis, Vance's salary exceeds one hundred thousand dollars a year, and is growing.

"I used to head up fundraising," LaVerne says, "but I don't do that either."

I ask why.

"I don't know what the money is going to, and I have to be able to sleep at—he's back!"

The wren hops between the branches, another worm in his mouth, but this one is still alive.

⁖⁖⁖⁖⁖

Since the CBPP is a registered charity, its recent tax information is available online. The 2016 fiscal year was indeed devastating. Expenses exceed revenue by $122,955, despite the $52,000 the organization received in government funding. There is also the curious expenditure of $113,275 (over 9 per cent of their overall expense) categorized under "Political activities," a category which had been absent in the years prior.

The financial burden of the CBPP is unique. Unlike most other theatre companies, it caters to a clientele composed mainly of the political right, and the organization risks contravening the economic ideology of its base when its funding relies too heavily on government grants. Moreover, the acceptable relationship between corporate sponsorship and religious proselytizing has never been made clear. For example, Professional Model Jesus was also a real estate agent and used a picture of his crucified self on promotional materials: "Realtor With a Cause," his randomly capitalized RE/MAX business card read, "and That Cause is Christ."

Online, I look under "Compensation" and see there are two full-time employees making less than 40 K a year and one employee making between 40 and 80 K a year.

"Pilate is full of shit," I say to Maisy. "Vance is raking in eighty thousand, tops."

But I realize there are only two full-time employees at the CBPP: Vance and the Office Manager. I look at the tax records of the three previous years. Each one claims there were only two employees: one making under 40 K a year and one making between 80 and 120 K.

I look again at the dog. "Is Vance paying himself two salaries?"

⌗ ⌗ ⌗ ⌗ ⌗

Five years ago, a friend of mine got divorced and no longer needed his how-to-fix-a-marriage books, so he offered them to me.

"Free of charge?" I asked, flipping through the one with a Tolkien-like ring on the cover.

But I was always too ashamed to read them. They sat untouched on my shelf, the only books with their spines facing the wall, until this past week, with Diabolos waiting in his idling Volkswagen, when I frantically searched for a book to bring with me but realized everything I wanted to read—*Death in Venice, A Passage to India, The Collected Stories of Herman Melville*—was about gay sex. A car horn honked, and I grabbed one of the marriage books, figuring that the Passion play's campground would be the perfect place to read it: the riverside solitude would afford me the reflection needed, and if I were discovered, the book's subject matter would imply not only that Litia and I are married (we're not) but also that I uphold the institution as a lifelong bond (most Christians believing that a broken marriage is nothing that several decades of unhappiness can't fix).

My next time off in Calgary, I suggested to Litia that we vow to take more of an interest in the other's job, and she agreed. "You thought of this?" she asked.

I said yes, and it was only when she did not know I was lying that I realized how gifted a thespian I had become.

For me, this vow means brainstorming lesson plans and helping hang classroom decorations. For her, it means buying a wide-brimmed hat, because as I have repeatedly warned her, the Promised Land is very hot.

In addition to teaching grade one, Litia works as a photographer and has agreed to snap some pictures of the cast for my later reference. As she drives me and the dog to Drumheller, I describe what I want her to capture. "Some of these people," I say, "have this strange, carnival beauty that I don't know how to put into words."

"Strange, carnival beauty?" she echoes.

"Yeah," I say. "People you'd be chased by through a house of mirrors." Litia takes her eyes off the road for a good five or six seconds to look at me. "Are you, like, getting into character?"

We descend into the valley, passing the statue of the golden T-Rex who waves his tiny arms at the sandstone sign that reads, *WELCOME TO DRUMHELLER*. We're tailgated by a pickup truck that has swerved onto the highway off a dirt road, two men sitting in the flatbed. A group of children, no older than twelve, skulk outside Jerry's Cold Beer and Wine, smoking. A woman walking on the side of the road plays paddleball with herself.

"It was named after a coin toss," I tell Litia.

"The town?"

"Yeah. There were two coal miners, Samuel Drumheller and Something Greentree, who bet the naming rights on a coin toss."

We pass the vandalized storefront of Fred and Barney's Family Restaurant, now abandoned.

"Who won?"

"Who won? What do you mean who won? Drumheller won."

Litia turns left at the lights, and we pass the fertilizer store, the tire store, and the store that I'm not really sure what kind it is because —according to its signage—it only sells "petroleum and twine." We pass the plastic fabrication plant, the diesel truck repair shop, the Dinosaur Hotel. Oilfield services, industrial supplies, fast food.

And it occurs to me what Litia was asking: If there was a chance that Greentree called "heads" and watched the coin spin before landing to show the upturned face of his bearded sovereign, and then Greentree surveyed his surroundings, took in what the future promised, and said to his friend, "This is all on you."

<hr />

Before Litia is allowed to take pictures, Vance has insisted on meeting with us. His office has somehow become even messier, to the point of conceptual art: a bottle of hot sauce oozing atop a VHS tape; a framed picture of a dagger resting inside a file folder; a pad of paper with only the word *YES!* scrawled across it. In the corner, an air conditioner roars with such force that the Nicaraguan flag on the opposite wall flutters in its breeze.

"Lydia," Vance says. "Welcome."

Much like *quinoa*, Litia's name does not translate well from the written to the spoken word, and so she has grown patient yet precise in the correction of its pronunciation. "Lih-tee-ah," she tells Vance, pausing for him to take note. "And it's nice to be here."

"We are no strangers to media. Have you seen the Phil Spink documentary?"

Litia says, "What's that?"

Over the course of the summer, I have heard a lot about Phil Spink and his documentary. I wasn't able to find the documentary online or in the library, so Judas begrudgingly leant me his personal copy after making me promise to return it promptly and in its original condition.

The documentary is a feature-length film about the celebrated Gospel of John script of seven years past, but most of its run-time is spent asking questions like, "If Jesus drove a truck, what truck would that be?"[17] The Jesus in the documentary had a mad-scientist take on the role, but the understudy that year was cast as the lead in subsequent seasons and went on to become the Best Jesus Ever.[18] Aside from seeing that Barrett used to sport a Cleopatra hair bob, the most interesting part of the movie is when Vance casually admits to the camera that "everyone in the organization is carrying some of the load on credit cards, buying the things we need. And as those tickets sell, we're reimbursing and eking through. It's bonkers."

"Phil Spink really got this place," Vance tells Litia. "And we know that your husband will as well."

"I'm sure," she says.

"Because before Phil Spink, media came here and only made fun of us."

The CBPP has been subject to a handful of articles. And aside from those written by the *Drumheller Mail*, these articles are always cursory in their analysis, often with a hint of derision, most times commenting on nothing more than the novelty of the play's plot or the amazement that a real live donkey is trotted onstage. A documentary prior to Spink's had a pair of singing hillbillies for narrators, one with a cymbal on his head. An American academic paper derides the company for not casting Simon of Cyrene (who the Scriptures say is Ethiopian) as a person of colour and then suggests the directors remedy this by putting the white actor in blackface. A newspaper column from two seasons ago hit a particularly sour note within the cast when it was written in a style usually reserved for refugee crises:

---

17   The answer, for the record, is a triple-axel articulated dump truck with a rated payload of forty-five metric tons, according to Cassius, who was (coincidentally) Drumheller's local dump truck salesman.

18   In regard to the Best Jesus Ever, Pilate once told me, "If you would have asked me ten years ago my thoughts on him, I would have told you he is one of the douchiest human beings I've ever met. When I first heard he was to play Jesus, I was like, 'Are you fucking kidding me?' The taste of his fucking name in my mouth was vulgar. But then I came to work with him and I was like, 'He's really good.' The guy is skilled. He's seriously skilled."

"[I]n the hot desert sun, actors in thick woollen costumes routinely collapse from heat stroke. Characters are lashed to poles, thrown down stairs, dunked underwater and forced to jog for kilometres."

"So Laticia," Vance says. "We are okay with you taking photos, but I want to make sure we're on the same page."

He means a literal page and has the Office Manager print off a contract stating that the company reserves the right to veto any photos they wish.

"We are very uncomfortable with this," I say. "As a professional photographer and a professional — you know — book writer, I don't think we can agree to that."

"I know all about writing a book," Vance says, and from one of the many boxes behind him, he pulls out a paperback. Then, from a larger box, he pulls out another.

Vance, it turns out, is the author of two self-published novels: *The Scroll: Bringing Ancient Wisdom to Life* and *The Hammer: The True Danger Lies Within*.

"The best part about *The Hammer*," Vance says, "is the little hammer on the top right of each page spins if you flip through."

I do as instructed and watch the hammer twirl.

"I paid thousands to have that edited," Vance adds, "but I think I liked my original version more."

I place the novel on his desk, wedging it between a box of tissues and an empty can of soda.

"But that's me," Vance says, reclining deeply in his chair. "I'm a bit of a rogue. Like, I just spent three thousand dollars on Gabriel's wings. You think the board was happy with that?"

I marvel at the man's ability to spend inordinate amounts of money (whether it be his or not) on an artistic vision he believes in.

"People said I shouldn't let you in here," he continues, "because we only get taken advantage of. But then —" and Litia interrupts.

"Phil Spink."

"Phil Spink," he says. "And, I'm a bit of a rogue."

He tells a story about how, during his first year as executive director, he reduced the width of each seat by half, effectively doubling the amphitheatre's capacity. City Hall, however, had issues with the drastic increase of persons within a confined space. "I thought we were out here in the hills," he says, "and 'fire codes'"—he does the air quotes—"didn't affect us. It turns out, they do. But I'm a bit of a rogue."

I look at my watch. Rehearsal started thirty minutes ago. We are re-choreographing the genealogy sequence.

"Tell me more," I say.

In response to last year's shortcomings, Vance offered disgruntled patrons a money-back guarantee on this year's performance. This maverick promise could equal over $10,000 in refunded revenue.

The organization's bank account is empty, and this year's budget has already been blown on new fishing boats, a sundeck for Simon Peter, and Gabriel's four-figure, three-metre wingspan.

"All I want is magic," Vance says. "I didn't get magic last year. This year, I want magic."

"Magic?" I say. "Or a miracle?"

I meant it as a genuine question, but Vance laughs me off. "Ladia," he says, "my hands are tied."

Litia, who has started scrolling through old photos on her camera, realizes he's talking to her and says, "Okay."

She pushes aside a tangle of unset mousetraps to make a small clearing on the desk. As she signs on the line, I read the contract's first term of reference: "The photos are going to be used in articles/books that portray the rehearsal process and the making of the Passion Play (similar to Phil Spinks [*sic*] documentary)."

Vance signs the contract too. His signature isn't so much an autograph as it is the tell-tale lines on a lie detector.

Litia and I leave the office, exiting into a sunlight so severe it hits like pepper spray.

"Why is he being so protective?" I ask Litia.

Our eyes adjust, and she takes a picture of the parking lot, but the light is so bright the camera screen only shows beige. "You know why," she says and lets loose a long whistle. Maisy—who has been curled in the soft grass beneath the Stage Manager's trailer—bounds across the lot.

In the amphitheatre, Litia shoots pictures of the cast as we get ready to run the first act.

"Oh my gosh," she whispers. "Is that Jesus?"

"Kind of," I say. "That's His understudy." Jesus Understudy is standing in a pocket of sunlight that cuts across the battlements of the set. Everyone is whirlpooling around him, hurriedly getting ready. And in this light, he does seem conspicuously Christ-like—not just because of the abundant physical similarities (his summer skin has acquired a gorgeous Palestinian hue) but also the gentle sorrow that radiates from him, like a taxidermic deer or a statue behind the altar of a church filled only by tourists.

I point to the real Jesus, texting behind the water cooler, and Litia peers through her viewfinder to zoom in. She shakes her head. "Too Italian."

"Lay off," I say. "He's been on *Supernatural*."

She snaps a picture of the Lord, but unbeknownst to her, a Villager (one with a strange, carnival beauty) sits in the background and has inserted her middle finger far into her nose, her mouth slightly agape. I peer over her shoulder at the camera's screen. "Perfect," I whisper. "That's going to be the cover."

"No," she says, beeping her way to the delete button. "It's not. And I think you've spent enough time getting into character."

‹ SCENE 12 ›

Co-director Jessica and I are reading the laminated menu at Drumheller's Vietnamese Noodle House, wedged between a Baptist church and the Tastee-Delite ice cream shop. There is exactly one vegetarian option: "White roll," the server tells me, and I am unsure if he means the roll is white or is for white people.

I wanted to speak to Jessica because I have surmised that she is not religious. Not only does she live in the hedon-haven of Vancouver Island, but she did not bow her head during last Friday's lunchtime prayer, something I only noticed because I wasn't bowing my head either. I have prepared a lengthy inquisition to get her to admit her secularity — something with Obadiah trivia and recitations of the Song of Solomon — but she confirms my suspicions readily.

"I did go to church when I was really, really young," she says, "and it was so boring." (Obviously, her church was not affiliated with the Christian sleep-away camp I summered at as a child.) "Last night, a cast member was telling me, 'This must be really great for your résumé.' And I was like, 'Well, sort of. If someone is a Christian in Victoria, and I come across that person, they might have heard of it. But most people don't even know what a Passion play is.'"

"Someone once asked me," I say, leaning in, "'Aren't all plays passionate?'" and together we giggle at the brimstone that awaits the unaware hordes.

Jessica first came to the Passion play through a posting on an actors' union job board. After this year's production, she will have helped direct the show for three separate seasons, to a combined audience of more than forty-five thousand souls.

"Before you started at the Passion play," I ask, "how did you imagine Jesus?"

"All the clichés," she says. "A white guy, with a beard, surrounded by other white people. And flowing robes, for sure."

These clichés are alive and well within the CBPP, particularly in regard to the North Pole whiteness of the actors. Moreover, thanks to the unparalleled mastery of the costume department, the cast's flowing robes are exceptionally arresting—Caravaggio-esque—and I have spent entire afternoons hypnotized by the tattered strands of Demon Possessed Woman's kaftan coiling in the summer breeze.

"I was quite nervous my first year," she says, "because I was worried I was going to be challenged. My first year, Pharisee with Cane wouldn't take direction from me."

Aside from this season's scandal being a female Holy Spirit, Jessica says there has also been pushback to casting female angels, and dressing the male angels in rose gold and baby blue.

"But pushback is to be expected," she says. "When you sign up to be in *Seussical,* it's not going to test your beliefs."

Our meal arrives, and my roll is indeed both white and for white people: white rice paper wrapped around white rice noodles and white bean sprouts. "Not too spicy," the server tells me, smiling. He points to a jar of hot sauce sitting on the table. "Very spicy," he says, his face dark and sombre. "Very, very spicy."

Jessica worked another contract last summer, so this is her first time with the new script. I ask if she likes the play.

"It's hard," she says, and her voice gets an octave higher with each ensuing sentence: "It's an interesting one. It's very different. I think there's a lot of threads that I'm not 100 per cent sure what their purpose is."

"Like what?"

"At the beginning of the season," she says, "we had no idea what the Holy Spirit's role was. How does She affect Jesus? How does She affect everyone else? Gabriel, we haven't figured out yet. I just don't know what his role is in this script. And are the voice-overs the best way to tell this story? And the Dark Angels—what *are* they?"

She takes a breath. "I don't doubt that it is a good show. But I think we have a few more years to finesse it."

Now that we have begun rehearsing the second act, I have grown increasingly concerned that nobody aside from those fluent in the Bible will appreciate our play. This is especially troubling since not many Christians have read the Good Book either. "How long did Jesus stay alive after coming back from the dead?" I overheard one teenage Villager ask another in the lineup for iced tea. "Three days," the other Villager answered. "Or maybe it's a week—Sunday to Sunday. No, wait—forty days. Isn't that what Lent is? When God *lent* us His Son."

Even senior members of the cast are perplexed: "Which of you is older?" Jessica asked Jacob and Isaac during a recent rehearsal of the genealogy sequence, and the father-son combo answered with slack-jawed silence.

Jessica, however, believes that a large portion of our audience is secular. "People come for the spectacle," she says. "People come up to me after the show to say they're non-religious."

It seems strange to me that someone would weave their way through the play's exiting rush just to approach one of the co-directors and say, "I do not believe in eternal life," but it seems even stranger to believe that a non-religious person would have the slight-est idea what is happening onstage. Why, pray tell, does Jesus sweat blood in the Garden of Gethsemane? Why does Pontius Pilate kill Judas in one scene only to have Judas enter in the next? Why does a voice-over of the Holy Spirit whisper to Christ, "Receive My power," and Jesus suddenly possesses the ability to Jedi-forcefield Diabolos?

Since my scenes have been going prodigiously well, I sat with Litia in the audience as Barrett fine-tuned the play's troubled sections. "I thought you people didn't believe in cavemen," Litia whispered to me upon spotting John the Baptist in his camel cloak. Then, witnessing the Angel Choir splendid in their rose gold and baby blues, she asked, "Why is Gabriel dressed like a unicorn?"

I thought Litia's assumption that the harbinger of Christ is half angel, half horned horse was as bad as it could get, but then she watched Scene 22c: The Transfiguration, where Christ hikes up a mountain and is visited by apparitions.

"Is that Father Time?" she said, referencing a spirit's elegant robe, gnarled staff, and unbound mane of silver hair.

"Are you high?" I whispered. "It's Elijah."

"What's his power?"

"Power? He's not a superhero. He's a prophet. He foretold the future."

"And there's not an X-Men who does that?"

"This is a *Passion* play."

"Which reminds me," she said, "aren't all plays passionate?"

In the restaurant, my meal tastes exactly like how the word *white* sounds. I open the jar of hot sauce, and from the smell alone, my eyes bloom into red and poisonous flowers.

I ask Jessica how the directing team is dealing with the stress of living in the shadow of last year's financial failure.

"I wasn't sure that people knew that," she says.

"Everyone knows," I say.

The other night at O'Shea's, Pontius Pilate and Judas parsed the prior season's shortcomings. "Financially," Pilate said, "last year didn't go well because we didn't market it worth a shit."

Judas, whom O'Shea's short-skirted staff positively swooned over despite his only ever ordering ice water, placed the blame on a narrative unbalance: "It took forty-five minutes to get to adult Jesus."

Pilate nodded. "There was a lot of dragging ass."

"We started with the genealogy sequence," Judas said, "and it took a while. It then went into bridesmaids talking, and, oh look, there's Mary, and Mary gets visited by Gabriel, and then she goes with Joseph, and then Joseph has to get it inn, and he can't get it inn"—I'm unsure if the double entendre is intentional or Freudian—"so he gets a stable, and they go to the stable."

"And then we had an angry British guy come out," Pilate said, "and he's like, 'I ain't got no room.' And they're like, 'But we need a room.' And he's like, 'Tuff shite, I ain't got no room.'"

There have been edits to this year's script, but Judas is still sceptical about the pacing. "It's not a clean-focused story," he said. "Simon Peter starts the play with, 'Empty nets, empty purse,' whine-whine-whine. And then Jesus dies, and he has the exact same whiny, bitchy shit right after, meaning the last two and a half hours didn't impact him at all."

These misgivings are especially disheartening because, at last count, the play was running *three* and a half hours.

Jessica devours her final roll, something delicious and surf 'n' turfy, bright shrimps glowing through the rice paper. "It has been stressful," she says, "with that ever-looming cloud of 'It Needs to Be Good.' But when I see our show, I can't imagine wanting my money back. It's such a spectacle."

"Isn't there a version of this play that is an assured success?" I ask. "A God who is a white male, with a Holy Spirit who is a white male, with a Jesus who is a white male, totally not gay, doing stuff with His buddies—not gay. A Jesus who is wildly charismatic, compassionate, definitely not gay. Why aim to add art to a show whose patrons don't want it?"

"I think they do," she says. "In the age of movies with multi-million-dollar budgets, I mean, you go watch *Wonder Woman* and then the Passion play needs to compare."

"Jessica," I say, "you think the people who watch the Passion play have seen *Wonder Woman*?"

Only from her recoil do I realize how dismissive I have become. Like somebody can't enjoy both X-Men and Elijah. Indeed, once, didn't I?

Behind the restaurant's till, the teenage hostess cranks up the radio: Lady Gaga's "Just Dance." Jessica takes her last, perfectly seasoned bite, and I ask if she considers herself a feminist.

"I'm not like —" she says, raising a clenched fist.

"What does this mean?" I say, repeating the gesture.

"I mean, I don't go to rallies," she says, "but I think I am."

"Do you think the Passion play is a patriarchal environment?"

In relation to the script, she admits that most female characters have been sidelined to male storylines. "But in the directing team, I've never felt my voice is less than someone else's."

"Then why does Barrett always speak after you when you two address the cast?"

"Barrett and I have talked about this, and it's because he finishes with something faith-based."

"The cast prays," I say, "like, all the time. How many times do you think a woman has led that prayer?"

"Maybe three?"

"Zero."

"No," she says, "Midwife 3 led it once."

"I must have missed that," I say.

"What I notice," she says, "is that it's always the same three or four people. Like, give someone else a chance."

"But isn't that the definition of a patriarchal society?"

She shrugs. And what am I supposed to do? Tell her that what she believes is wrong despite her having lived it? At some point, the path of logic and belief inevitably forks. And is it better to slow-clap the enlightenment of those who take the former route or to envy the wide-eyed wonder of those who elect the latter? I shrug back.

At the start of June, there was a stage combat call for the rehearsal of Scene 12: Calling of Simon Peter / Parable of the Lost Son. The scene concludes with Jesus crowd-surfing out of His fishing boat into the waiting arms of the seaside village. The crowd who assembled to perform the hoisting was composed of able-bodied men—which is why I found myself in the cafeteria with Mary Magdalene, Joanna, and Susanna, who, along with Mother Mary, compose the entirety of the play's mortal and multi-scene female characters. As we drank Twinings Earl Grey and morning-old coffee, I asked them their thoughts on the objections to a female Holy Spirit. "Pharisee with Cane," I said, "called it a New Age-y attack."

In astounding unison, they rolled their eyes.

"Typical," Susanna said.

"What's the big deal if the Holy Spirit is a girl?" Joanna added. "Like, do people really think the Holy Spirit has a…you know."

Mary Magdalene stared into her paper cup. "The Holy Spirit is a *spirit*. It's right there in the name."

Midwife 3 was seated at the table behind us, studying her lines. I could tell by how her irises stayed still that she was no longer reading. Also, she doesn't have any lines.

"But doesn't that same logic apply to God?" I asked Mary Magdalene. "What's making Him a *Him*?"

"Sometimes," Susanna said, her eyes smouldering like lanterns turned low, "when I'm speaking with God, He is a woman."

For a non-religious person, it is difficult to understand how subversive this sentiment is. Historically speaking, God has been male for longer than Earth has revolved around the Sun. To call Him a Her is not simply an expanding of definition—it concedes a level of asininity within those who have written the foundations of faith. Because if God isn't a dude, why has He been such a bro: employing only men as popes, enshrining the ownership of wives within the Ten Commandments, and declaring the use of condoms a mortal sin?

Mary Magdalene nodded. Joanna was in such agreement that she raised her paper cup in a gesture of "hear, hear."

Midwife 3 closed her script and shook her head.

I asked the three women what they'd think if next season's Jesus were cast as a female. Mary Magdalene chewed her lip. "But the Bible says Jesus was human. And humans have to either be a man or a woman."

"What's the difference?" Susanna said. "You think He was actually white? But we have no problem pretending He was. Jesus being *human* is the important part. Who cares if He is She?"

Midwife 3 took Susanna's question as an invitation and approached our table. "Such an interesting conversation," she told us through a shark-like smile. "But the Bible clearly says 'He' in reference to the Holy Spirit, God, and His Son." She then echoed herself: "His *Son*."

"But isn't that just a translation thing?" Susanna said, and Midwife 3's smile widened. God's male gender is a product of English translation, since English doesn't have a gender-neutral pronoun. However, as Temple Guard 4 pointed out to me, in the Hebrew Bible, the pronoun used to refer to the Holy Spirit is feminine.

"It's fun to imagine," Midwife 3 said, her smile inflating to carnivorous proportions. "But imagining can get you into trouble."

Outside came a raucous clamour: the cast had either lifted the Lord or dropped Him.

In my previous, hedonistic life, I would end each interview with the question: "Do you have any questions for me?" However, in my current life of theatrical religiosity, I've done away with that question for fear I would be asked, "Do you believe in God?" But as Jessica and I wait for the bill, she asks, "Are you enjoying being in the play?" and somehow this question is even more complicated.

I say that the play has a tenderness I never expected, that we are beautifully reminiscent of *A Midsummer Night's Dream*: our little group of mechanicals, rehearsing in the thickets, planning our big show, and wringing our hands white with worry that no one will come.

"But," I tell her, "at some moments, I feel profound loneliness. I feel I've really connected with somebody, and then something comes up—like bike lanes—and it shows how far apart we are."

It is true that the Canadian Badlands Passion Play is one of the kindest, most welcoming environments I have ever been in. Like when, without my asking, Clarinet Player halves her granola bar with me even though the day has been long and brunch quite meagre; or when Doubting Thomas lends me his script when I have forgotten mine, damning himself to be woefully lost for the rest of rehearsal; or when I approach Diabolos at the campfire and, my eyes welted with tears, ask if he thinks it is possible for someone to be born without a soul, and he, with neither hesitation nor reflection, puts his hand on my knee and says, "Never heard something so silly."

It is also true that the Canadian Badlands Passion Play is one of the cruellest. Chuza tells me he's reading a book that proves Christians are responsible for all positive aspects of civilization, everything from hospitals to universities, aqueducts to post offices. Wealthy Herod Guest 2 tells me it is morally wrong that Litia is physically stronger than me since I will therefore be unable to protect her. Herbalist declaims that unwed partners should be barred from church, a barring which would include none other than Wealthy Herod Guest 2 and his presumedly anemic girlfriend, new Martha of Bethany.

But ever since I agreed to spend all summer with Jesus H. Christ, who repeats ad nauseam that we shall all be judged, I have realized how inept I am at separating good from bad—the two now striking me as inextricable.

‹ SCENE 13 ›

Sunday's rehearsal, and we spend all morning practising the genealogy sequence. The script calls for a rainbow to appear after Noah's flood, but thus far one has not appeared. "What happened to the rainbow?" I ask the Stage Manager.

"Can you hold on a second?" she says into her headset. She looks at me. "What?"

I point to the stage direction in the script: *A rainbow appears.*

"Oh, that was never going to happen on this stage."

"But didn't Barrett write this script *for* this stage?"

The Stage Manager presses her earpiece into her ear. "Say that again," she says, walking away, and I am doubtful if there is anyone on the other end.

I slouch over to Litia. She says, "I thought you were Herod."

"I am."

"Why don't you ever rehearse those scenes?"

I had been wondering this myself lately; due to the triage of the play's more troublesome sections, my Herodian scenes have largely fallen by the wayside. I do, however, continue to wear the beige dress day in, day out.

"It's quite common," I tell Litia, "to not rehearse a script's most central scenes. Don't want to overplay perfection."

We run the genealogy sequence, and our choreography is sloppy to the point of peril: Gabriel is late carrying Adam's lifeless body downstage and causes a pile-up; Maleleel misses his mark and is elbowed in the side of the head by Lamech; Salah turns counterclockwise around the fire and nearly clotheslines Nahor with his sceptre.

We are supposed to spiral upon Abraham's altar and, after a few brisk bars of interlude, step back to reveal a miraculously constructed throne. But Cainan never has enough time to align the backrest's rare-earth magnets, and so for the fifth run-through in a row David, King of Israel, is forced to squat above a collapsing chair like a backpacker above an unclean toilet.

Taking the stairs two at a time, Jessica marches down from the amphitheatre's aisle. "We've been at this all summer," she tells everyone (but especially Methuselah). "Say. Your. Name. On. The. Beat."

The Fight Director takes Cain aside because he is still stabbing Abel with a windmill approach.

"Okay, people," the Musical Director hollers. "I've got a good feeling about this one. Let's take it from the Holy Spirit's line"—and then, in a sing-song falsetto—"God SAW the PEOPLE on EARTH and that EVERYTHING they THOUGHT and PLANNED were EVILLLL."

The soundtrack cues, the Holy Spirit croons, the thunder roars, ribbons of fire dance in the torches. And Noah brings it all crashing down by forgetting his own name.

At lunch, the cafeteria holds the ambience of purgatory, everyone milling around, eyes on our sandals, fretful of how our futures will play. I beg Litia to leave her sloppy joe half-eaten and drive me to the gas station.

"Can't you drive yourself?" she asks.

I am still worried about leaving her alone with the cast, that they'll be able to smell her original sin. "What if someone asks who your favourite disciple is?"

"Used to be Simon," she says, nodding at Simon Peter holding court in the hallway, "now it's Garfunkel."

Opening night is seven days away, and the temperature has sweltered to the mid-thirties. Under this combination of stress and heat, I have reverted to a diet of ultra-light cigarettes and Tropical Mango Powerade—the same diet I implemented before my maiden colonoscopy.

In the gas station's parking lot, I unwrap the cellophane, bite out a cigarette, and hand Litia the package.

"Do people in the cast know you smoke?" she asks.

"I don't smoke," I say, the cigarette pinched between my lips. I strike one of the cashier's matches but only skin the sulphur.

"What are you doing?" Litia demands, grabbing the matchbook. "We're at a gas station."

"It's different here," I say.

"*It* being fire?"

I point to a man filling up his F-450, a pair of metallic testicles dangling from the hitch. The man holds the pump with his right hand; with his left, he is smoking a Colt cigar.

"Just be thankful he isn't idling," I tell Litia, grabbing the matchbook back.

The match catches, and I inhale deeply. The smoke fills my body like a soul. Litia shrugs and places a cigarette between her own lips. She leans towards me, holds her hands on either side of my face, and we kiss through the tips of our cigarettes.

Sometimes, I have these moments where I take a half-step back from my life and it all seems so surreal, so alien, so hodgepodged together that it can't be my life at all but rather some slapdash skit being performed by a beginner improv troupe. In these moments, life becomes art—not necessarily in the sense that it's beautiful, but in the sense that it's experienced, evaluated, and (if I'm lucky) understood. Moments that blindside, and I stumble out of myself— ever so slightly—to realize how glorious and absurd this world is:

Litia, in her cutoffs, the sunshine like white irises on her sunglasses, with her hair ponytailed back to show her jaw cantilever as she takes a pull off the cigarette, all the while the smell of gasoline curls through the air; and then the F-450 shakes into ignition (and the sunglasses' irises are revealed to be not the sunshine but the sunshine's reflection off the chrome scrotum as it sways), and the driver cracks his window to let loose a tight stream of AC as he flicks his cigar butt that twirls, slow-motion, coming to land in a dark puddle before our feet. And then there's that secret thanks of believing the apocalypse has finally arrived.

Since arriving at the Passion play, I have realized that the very religious will experience these moments, at a minimum, once a week—usually on a Sunday. Last Sunday at our campground, the poplar trees bloomed and their fat flakes of cotton pendulummed upon us, catching on our clothes and sunhats and the eyelashes of Bartholomew, and the world gifted us all of the softness of winter without any of its hardness.

Litia gasps and points to the southern ridge. "What is that?"

"That," I say, "is not a *that* but a *He*."

Above Drumheller towers a thirty-foot Jesus. But unlike Rio de Janeiro's Christ the Redeemer, who is erect with crucifix-like right angles, Drumheller's Jesus is keeling forward from the ankles, His arms off-kilter, in the final seconds before swan-diving off the cliff.

In the 1960s and '70s, local artist Trygve (Tig) Seland sculpted thirty dinosaur statues to cash in on Drumheller's Jurassic past. (Tig also created the three giant geese in Hanna, Alberta; Eddie the Squirrel in Edson; and Aaron the Blue Heron in Barrhead: worthy day-trips, all.) Made of concrete and fibreglass, the dinosaurs were originally erected on the town's outskirts for an open-air museum named Prehistoric Park, where visitors were free to roam the hoodoos, dig for fossils, and stumble upon the stone-faced behemoths of the past.

The "cementosaurs" included a ghoulish Albertosaurus, a stegosaurus with scoliosis, and an unsettlingly human Trachodon. Straying from the confines of science, Tig also crafted a Smileasaurus Banana Eater and Shyasaurus Jelly Bean Eater. In their heyday, the cementosaurs obtained just enough success to make them offensive, prompting Tig's Creationist neighbour (name unknown) to construct the Jesus statue to watch over, and perchance convert, the apocryphal attraction.

Tig died in the late 1980s, and Prehistoric Park expired soon after, rendered extinct by Drumheller's new Royal Tyrrell Museum. The cementosaurs languished until City Hall established the Adopt-a-Dinosaur program, pairing local businesses with dinosaur statues on their street corners. However, the Jesus statue (or the "Cementossiah") was believed to only drive customers away, and His exile in the hills was upheld. Also, and for reasons which have never been made clear, a pterodactyl remained as well. So the mid-flight reptile, kennelled behind temporary fencing, keeps company with the Lord: a lone pirate and His parrot.

※ ※ ※ ※

The afternoon's rehearsal continues our bad luck. The smoke bombs for Diabolos' temptation of Christ aren't detonating on cue, and the body doubles of both the Devil and the Lord are three-quarters of the way through their hilltop scene when a whizzbang blows mere metres in front of them. The body doubles flinch, but since their lines are being voiced by a pre-recorded Diabolos and Jesus, they must push through their blocking.

"Ah, you are right," the voice of Diabolos says, as his body double makes t'ai chi–sized gestures. "And wise. There is a better kind of food." Another whizzbang, this time from their right, and the two enemies become comrades on the field of battle.

The actual Diabolos is backstage. The Head of Wardrobe is re-pinning his wings, which are black and stubby and not staying erect. He senses the cast's despair. "It'll turn around," he says. "We need to have faith."

But even he has a despondency about him. The Head of Wardrobe finishes her work, removes her hands, and both wings slump against his back.

Lunchtime at the campground, and as the potluck line files forward, I try to take note of the eyes of my fellow thespians. I can almost do it in the solstice light, when the day is nowhere near over

121

but exhaustion has snaked itself in: the crow's feet, the sunglass tan, the eyeliner of dirt.

The line shuffles along, and on the train of picnic tables, I notice that this is the first week all summer where mine is not the only vegetarian dish. A Dark Angel slides a cookie sheet of spanakopita across the table. She winks at me, and I am breathless with thanks.

My bliss redoubles when I see someone has brought potato salad with bacon *on the side*.

"Here," Lead Drummer says, taking two shish kebabs segregated on his BBQ tray. "These don't have chicken on them." He hands me both skewers. "Which is what you like, right?"

For a moment, words do not come. I nod to shake one loose. "Yes," I say, and hunger has become an incredible gift.

⊔ ⊔ ⊔ ⊔ ⊔

Evening, and Litia drives me and the dog through the light industrial park, spotted with welding supply stores, vacant warehouses, and a bus bench with no advertising. The property of the old Prehistoric Park (and, by extension, Giant Jesus and His pterodactyl) is now owned by Valley Auto Recyclers, a pick-and-pull in the southwest corner of the city, just past Resurrection Paint Ball.[19] We turn onto a dirt road that bends through the coulees, where Litia parks behind a butte. I'm out of the door and struggling over a barbed wire fence while the dog trenches underneath. Litia takes a picture of the sign that reads *24 HOUR SURVEILLANCE*, and walks ten metres west to where the wire is already felled.

The evening's earlier storm has soaked into the topsoil, affording the ascent a treadmillish quality. I stumble and reach out to a bush of wild sage but rise punctured with cactus spikes. From the highway, the hike seemed easy, so Litia is wearing flip-flops. Halfway up, she says she'll wait for me atop a slab of sandstone.

The dog sees a gopher and bounds after.

---

19 Hand to God, its real name.

I pilgrimage on, alone.

These are troubled times for the cementosaurs. Now in an urban environment, they have become prey to Drumheller's feral and disaffected youth. What began as simple graffiti—often celebrating the many-headed virility of a certain triceratops—has escalated into violence reminiscent of the French Revolution. The favoured pastime is now noosing the neck of a cementosaur with a chain that is anchored to a truck's hitch (most likely removing a pair of metal testicles in the process). The beheading is announced by the squealing of tires and concludes with the sound of a cement skull, which turns out to be preciously delicate, fracturing across the asphalt.

According to the owners of Valley Auto Recyclers, Jesus draws His own share of hooligans, but the harm is not done to Jesus Himself but rather the vehicles that neighbour Him. There are weekends where the scrapyard has awoken to over $10,000 of damage: car batteries through windshields, motorbikes driven over hoods, nights where every car door has been taken. And something about this destruction seems especially bitter, the "try and stop me" arrogance spewed at the statue.

The scrapyard tried to sell Christ online to finance a fence around the property, but the deal fell through. Professional Model Jesus and his Mother Mary real-life wife considered turning the area into a Jerusalem amusement park, but that idea proved commercially unviable.

When I finally crest the ridge, I hear Christ before I see Him: the statue creaks in the wind that cuts across the prairie and swirls into the valley.

Jesus' face has been sculpted by an amateur. His eyes rest on different latitudes, and His nose is small and razor-sharp. He does not have lips. But most striking is His lightbulb-shaped head, which forces His brow to droop on the sides, giving Him the expression of great loneliness.

I walk behind Him and see His calves have caved in to reveal His wire armature. I poke my head inside the hollow body, and from high inside the statue's chest, I hear roosting pigeons rustle. I shield my eyes from the coming scatter, but the birds do not emerge.

On behalf of the non-religious, I do not think we appreciate the Cassandra-like torture that the pious undergo on a day-to-day basis—believing that they have the answer to end all suffering, if only people would answer the doorbell. And then, too, is the taunting, the scoffing, the humiliation. Imagine the desperation that compels a man to try and save his neighbour's soul through the construction of a skyscraper Christ. "We have to get this right," Moses implores us during our afternoon pep talk. "Entire destinies *literally* hang in the balance."

In the broadest sense, an actor in the Canadian Badlands Passion Play is the man who stuccos your ceiling (Simon Peter) or the woman who pumps your gas (Baptizee 4) or the boy who bungees baseboard to your roof rack (Andrew the Apostle). They are those we have no problem not seeing. And so who of us, if rendered invisible, would not create something—or someone—to see us? Not in an abstract, he-knows-when-you're-sleeping sense but on a tangible, concrete level. To pluck a boy out of Vancouver who has a Nazarene quality about His brow and force Him to spend contractual hours staring into our eyes. What impels someone to sacrifice their entire summer, all to sing the lines "God saw the people of the earth, and everything they thought and planned were evil"? But perhaps the sorrow of the second half is overcome by the splendour of the first.

I wanted to join the Passion play because it would force me into a place where I would be given—at a minimum—a weekly opportunity to rise out of my solipsistic self and look upon this born-again congregation. And in seeing them, I wanted to know if I would see myself.

Sitting at the foot of the statue, I overlook southern Alberta. The storm clouds retreat into the neighbouring time zone, and I think to the last minutes of rehearsal: not wanting to fall even further behind schedule, we rehearsed through the rain, even when the showers turned torrential. The water drummed so loudly atop backstage's corrugated overhang that we couldn't hear our cues. "Herod!" the Assistant Stage Manager shouted, and I—my costume clinging like a wet T-shirt—clomped onstage to berate my manservant with a force I had not yet mustered.

I returned backstage to cower in Christ's old tomb, and I peered out to Servant Girl extending her hand into the overhang's rivulets, which spattered onto her palm. And past her, I saw Christ onstage, speaking to His followers. "Don't you know what spirit you belong to?" But then, as the directors called cut to debate whether it was too slippery for the pallbearers to carry the Boy of Nain's body down the cliffside, Jesus looked up to the clouds, snapping His fingers, and said, offscript, "Stop." And the rain indeed did stop, and the face of both Him and everyone around Him shone with rainbow-light, and the damp soil smelled like red wine, and the sprouts of wet sage exhaled their incense; but Servant Girl continued to reach, higher and higher still, and from her half-smile I could tell that she was seeing herself from a cumulus distance, on the same elevation of the final drops which would no longer touch her hand.

While we now think of *passion* as denoting a state of intense enthusiasm, the word derives from the Latin *pati*, meaning "to suffer." And that is the word, in every sense, I was looking for in our potluck lineup to describe the souls I was seeing through their stained glass windows. Passion: eyes brimming with it.

On our descent back to the car, Litia trails behind to take pictures of the prickly pears, their yellow flowers centred with stigmata. Suddenly, she lets out a terrible cry, and I turn to see her clinging to the lip of a crater that had been trapdoored by tumbleweeds.

"Hold on!" I holler, scrambling upwards as she clings to the edge of our mortal world. In the commotion, the pigeons shatter out of the hollow Christ, a tidal careening along the cliffside. And from such a distance, how glorious our lives must seem.

‹ SCENE 14 ›

After morning warm-up, the Stage Manager makes an announcement: "Alrighty, everyone. Small change of plans. We're going to practise the sheep sacrifice a couple times before we start with the rest of rehearsal."

"Again?" Herbalist says. "You men are killing those sheep every day."

Jessica always participates in morning warm-ups; Barrett, however, believes warm-up to be beneath him and peers down at us from the benches of the fourth row, his well-gelled cowlick like the brim of a baseball hat against the sun.

He catches me staring. "How you doing, Herod?" he says, dropping exhausted onto the bench. He is wearing a T-shirt that reads, *Saskatchewan: Keep it Rural!*

According to Pilate, at the end of last season's collapse, Barrett went to Vance and gave him an ultimatum: "Either hire me as director or I'm taking my script and going home."

"The Luke script," Pilate said, "is all about the glorification of Barrett." If such be true, glory comes at a high cost.

I sit beside him. "You got a minute?"

"I've got as many as this lasts," he says, nodding to the stage, where Jessica has assembled her gang of Galilean Men, each of them holding a rope leash attached to a sheep.

"How are you liking this season?" I ask.

"It's going well," he says. "We're a bit behind in some areas, but it always comes together."

"Except for last year," I say.

He does not take the bait.

126

Over the course of the summer, a pattern has emerged within the co-director team: Barrett directs the scenes that have main characters, like Jesus, Simon Peter, or me; Jessica directs the scenes that feature those lost to the annals of history, like the singing Fishermen, or the sacrificing of the sheep, or the genealogy sequence. When there is a mix of the two within one scene, like my bocce ball scene, Barrett will direct Pilate, Maisy, and me, while Jessica takes charge of Wealthy Herod Guests 1 through 3 and my entourage of attendants. Depending on the day, either or neither will direct Chuza. The result of this division (whether intentional or not) is that there's a prestige to working with Barrett, that you matter; working with Jessica, on the other hand, means you are a nobody—a realization that hits hard for those who assumed otherwise.

"We need more energy from all of you," Jessica tells her actors. A Galilean Man crouches down to scratch his sheep's ears. The sheep baas, and the Galilean Man does too—both of them drowning out their director.

I ask Barrett if, in writing the script, he most valued narrative development or Biblical accuracy.

"Narrative," he says.

"Wait," I say. "What?"

He nods.

I had so expected him to say Biblical accuracy, I am caught without a follow-up. "I didn't think you'd admit that."

He nods again.

"Because even the most liberal actors here think that's wrong."

He smiles—not a lot, but it's there. "That," he says, "is why they need me."

Throughout the CBPP's life, Barrett has been around for longer than he hasn't. In 2004 and after the birth of his eldest daughter (now cast as Blind Woman's Child[20]), Barrett relinquished his command

---

20   While Blind Woman's Child is not herself blind, she does seem to possess superhuman hearing, to the extent that Pilate and I believe her to be Barrett's backstage mole. Living in genuine fear of her, we now gossip only in either Judas' trailer or the corner of the armoury's entrance, where the nearby garden hose provides enough white noise to ensure privacy.

of a touring theatre troupe and joined the Passion play in the role of Lazarus. The following year, the director of the show offered him the position of assistant director. Since then, he has steadily risen through the ranks until now he basically *is* the Canadian Badlands Passion Play, much like how Julius Caesar became synonymous with Rome. Last season, when Vance caved to Barrett's demand and granted him the directorship, Barrett insisted that Jessica return alongside him. Now he not only is the playwright and head of the directorial team but also enjoys the full support of some of the play's most vociferous volunteers. Simon Peter calls him his captain; the Virgin Mary rests her head upon his shoulder; Wealthy Herod Guest 2 says he is fantominal, even though that is not a word. During snack break, Diabolos speaks of him with deified reverence — "Did you see him catch that football?" he asked me after a rehearsal during which Barrett intercepted a pass from one Dark Angel to another. "Just incredible."

But even Caesar fell.

In the corner of the armoury's entrance, Pilate recently told me, "In all my years at the Passion play, I've never ever seen the cast so frustrated and divided." He was in his armour but wearing his fedora, and the armoury's lone lightbulb cast a film-noir shadow across his eyes. "So many angry people."

With a full month of rehearsals remaining, Judas won't even speak with Barrett anymore; the rough-and-tumble scenic arts crew openly mocks him; the entire wardrobe department (all five indefatigable women) are so upset that when we last went to Boston Pizza, they ranted against him until the manager — having already mopped, stacked the chairs, and turned off the AC — finally begged us to leave. Yet most worrisome to Barrett's security is the whole township of Villagers, the plebeian mass of the cast, that avoid him entirely, either out of fear or suspicion or utter apathy.

Sitting in the second row, I scuff my sandals in the dirt. "What do you think your relationship with the cast is like?"

Barrett shrugs. "What have you heard?"

I laugh.

So does he.

"I think my relationship with the cast is fine," he says. "There are some people who have issues with their character that are really just issues of ego."

And it is true: Pilate's animosity towards Barrett may not be as theologically based as Pilate would have me believe. Not only is Pilate still upset about having his reins confiscated for his entrance into Jerusalem, but Barrett and Jessica have recently announced the blocking for the play's finale: for the first time ever, the cast will not bow in the costumes of their primary character but rather dressed as nondescript Galileans. Instead of bowing in his splendid armour, Pilate is now taking his curtain call with a headscarf and large smock worn overtop his breastplate, a smock which makes him look like, by his own admission, a Ukrainian grandmother. "*Danke!*" he shouts, blowing kisses and confusing Ukrainian with German. "*Danke* you very much!"

There has been much debate about the end of the show, and two camps have emerged: the Jessica Camp, who want everyone dressed as nondescript Galileans; and the Pilate Camp, who want everyone to bow in their main character's costume. (Admittedly, there is a third camp—probably the largest—composed of the vast majority of actors whose main character is, in fact, a nondescript Galilean and who therefore don't care at all.)

The conflict between these two camps got to a point where a cast-wide meeting was called, during which Jessica sold her vision, saying that the message of the play is that we are all the same in God's eyes. The meeting ended with Pilate openly weeping.

"*Please* put this on fucking record," he told me, wiping his nose with the back of his hand. "This is one of the dumbest choices the directorial team of the Passion play has ever fucking made."

According to Judas, what is at stake is not just the bow but rather the conversations that actors have with audience members afterwards. "People come up to me after the show, and they know I'm not Judas, but you can kind of tell that they think I am. I've lost track of the amount of people who have approached me and said, 'Why did you do it?' And since I've spent months—years, now—with this character, I'm able to give them something of an answer."

Jesus Understudy forced himself into the conversation. "I saw it last year," he said, "this hunger in people's eyes. People looking at me, and I'm like, you think that I'm Jesus right now. People fly across the world for that."

"Yeah," Pilate said, taking a big sniff of snot. "And when Vance finds out that Jessica has axed the audiences' photo opportunities, he's going to fucking shit on his dick."

The Stage Manager interrupted us to ask if she could schedule an appointment between Pilate and the directors. Afterwards, I checked in with him.

"I got fucked over," he said. "Barrett sat quietly looking all fucking stoic. The Fight Director agreed with me on damn near fucking everything but didn't say anything. I told them that there was a whole bunch of people in the cast who felt the same way as me—at least fifteen other prominent members—and Jessica said, 'If these actors aren't here, why should we believe you?'"

The appointment concluded with the directors arbitrating a compromise: the cast will bow as nondescript Galileans; but those who wish can then return backstage, switch into their main character's costume, and go onstage to converse with the audience.

Pilate's camp quickly disbanded in defeat, but Pilate himself found a loophole. He decided not to take a bow at all—anonymous he would be within the Galilean mob—and instead would sit backstage in his armour, ready for his triumphal re-entry. He did this for several run-throughs, and nobody noticed, because there were bigger fish to fry (mainly, the interminable failures of the genealogy sequence). Eventually, I stayed with him, not because I was necessarily part of the Pilate Camp but because the hotter it became, the more my fingers swelled, and the more torturous it became to twist off my rings and force them on again.

One evening, Pilate and I sat backstage with Jesus, who bows after everyone else. The closing track played (an instrumental song featuring the enigmatic presence of African drums), and the three of us listened to the pitter-patter of stage management's applause.

"They're clapping in front of them," Pilate told me, "but we know who the real applause is for: you and me."

Jesus, who was texting, looked up.

"And you too," Pilate said.

Jesus nodded and went back to His phone, and the three of us sat smugly—our odd little trinity.

Pilate thought he'd won, until later that evening an email from the directorial team was circulated. Someone had ratted him out. The email said that those who do not participate in the bow cannot participate in subsequent photo opportunities.

"What are you going to do?" I asked him.

"I'll do the fucking bow," he said. "I *have* to talk with the audience. It means too much to too many people."

Belief in an empathetic God is the pinnacle of mortal hubris. Because faith and ego sprout from the same fruit: assuming that the Almighty cares about your problems. There is no humility in prayer, only the upturned mouths of baby birds wanting to be fed. And perhaps there is nothing more emblematic of the play's fall into the profane than Barrett, our own overlord, shrugging his shoulders at the pleas of the individual as he forces us forward, marching towards the glory of empire.

Barrett and I watch a Galilean man pretend to rodeo-ride a sheep even after Jessica has asked for focus. I ask Barrett if he believes the play is undergoing a gradual process of secularization in an attempt to draw a larger audience.

"There is a difference," he says, "between secularization and contemporization. We have to tell this story in a way that connects with people living now, not two thousand years ago."

"So you think the audience will be fine with how much of the story you've changed?"

Barrett was born in Ohio and studied theatre in New York City. "The thing I've noticed about Canadian audiences," he says, "is that they are really worried about what the person they brought with them thinks. I don't know what they'll think. All I can do is write what I think."

I ask if he ever wished he got a better Gospel, one of the fun ones, like Matthew or John.

"The Gospel of Luke is all about how to have a relationship with something that's not there. It's a hard theme—unpopular, even—but one we have to tell."

But Barrett, consumed by his all-encompassing vision, pays no heed to popularity. For example, he says that the script committee expressed serious reservations about having a female Holy Spirit. Barrett revised the script to obscure the role's gender, allowing the committee to grant approval as they tarried in male-normative assumptions until auditions, where he immediately cast a girl in order to interrogate those selfsame assumptions.

What the multi-million-dollar Passion plays of America all have in common is that, musical or not, they play only the hits. They know what the audience wants, and they deliver. As such, those productions aren't so much theatre as theatrical affirmations of already held beliefs. Barrett, on the other hand, has an artistic drive characterized by inversion, subversion, ambition. And lo, he is ambitious. His script is straight from the Golden Age of Hollywood, when directors were creators, when actors weren't cultural icons but emotional emancipators, when movies lasted longer than most insects live. But we no longer exist in that time. We exist in the era of cell phones, of wireless internet, of global temperatures so high that an unshaded amphitheatre in summer is a mortal gamble. We exist in the era of the snap-along musical.

For the first time, I begin to understand the immensity of the task before him: its scale, its sensitivity, but also its inevitable defeat. Because even if the show survives another year—or another ten—the play is indisputably in its twilight days, living off borrowed time.

During the quieter moments in the campground, when a group of us have stayed up late drinking Diet Pepsi and watching constellations of bats dart around the floodlight, even the most gung-ho of the cast concede that no script can ever top the Matthew version and no Jesus can ever out-act the Best Jesus Ever. In fact, the Best Jesus Ever continues to be so revered that his picture still hangs throughout the cafeteria, and both this and last season's Jesus are forced to eat brunch beneath the icon of all that they will never be.

Barrett talks to me about how, in just over a decade, the CBPP has gone from a public reading of the New Testament to a spectacle of smoke bombs and body doubles. Onstage at this very moment, a Galilean Man is half-heartedly dragging a blade across a sheep's esophagus.

"We need to evolve," he says. "Even the people who are against—as you put it—the secularization of the play know that we need to grow. Without that, we're dead."

Like the abandoned ski hill to our west and the abandoned Pre-historic Park to our east, it seems inevitable that one day (perhaps sooner than later) the great Wall of Jerusalem, the carved-out tomb of Christ, and the three onlooking crosses will be abandoned—graffitied and vandalized, visited only by trespassing tourists. And in imagining this, I am struck by a sudden sadness; how dull this world is, how hell-bent it is on crushing anything that deviates from the norm, until all we are left with are chorus lines and outdoor paintball.

"Energy," Jessica urges her sheep slayers.

"It's hot," one of them says.

"And these poor critters are wearing wool," says another.

"Baa," says the third.

"*Energy*," Jessica pleads. "When the Romans ambush you, you have to be scared."

"I'm scared of getting a sunburn," their leader says, and his posse laughs.

Jessica slams her fist against the Spice Trader's kiosk. "ENERGY!"

Even the sheep shut the fuck up.

The scene runs: efficient, electric, with a current of terror crackling underneath—the knives shining in the sunlight, the blood spraying across the stone.

冈冈冈冈

In Scene 30: Jesus Betrayed/Arrested, Simon Peter cuts off the ear of Servant of the High Priest during the scuffle to arrest Jesus and frogmarch Him to the Temple Guards. Backstage, Servant of the High Priest and I are watching through a doorway as Temple Guard Captain beats an unflinching Messiah. Servant of the High Priest crosses his arms and juts his chin at the Lord. "He gave me an acting note," he says. "He says I wasn't screaming enough."

We watch Temple Guard Captain—who has an unfortunate yet winsome speech impediment—interrogate Christ: "So, you awe not so special awe you, pwophet?"

Temple Guard Captain lands a right hook, but iron-jaw Jesus does not wince.

Servant of the High Priest shakes his head. "I'm like, Buddy, I've seen You being beaten, and let me tell You, *nobody* believes You."

Barrett is walking around the stage with the Fight Director to watch the beating from different angles. The other Temple Guards throw a barrage of haymakers, but the Lamb of God ingests each hit. Temple Guard Captain hurls a final uppercut, and Jesus is whiplashed by the punch; but then, like Rocky Balboa at the end of the fourteenth round, our Saviour rises—strong, solid, clown-faced with blood.

"The woosta," Temple Guard Captain says at the cock-a-doodle-doo sound cue. "Stand down, boys."

Scene 33b: Jesus Sent to Herod is the only scene I have with Christ, His last before being sentenced to death. My entrance for the scene comes from far stage left, through the backstage sound booth, where I await my cue by chatting with the On-Deck Sound Operator, who shares his salt water taffies.[21]

---

21   Herod's palace has no fixed point onstage but rather switches locations for each scene, wandering from centre stage to downstage right to upstage left. At first, I thought this choice signalled Barrett's artistic inconsistency, but I begin to see the choice as highly conceptual—that Herod's palace is not anchored to the temporal realm but is rather able to transverse any physical location, much like how we conceive of the soul. I voiced this idea to Pilate, and he, for the first and only time all summer, said nothing.

Today, however, the On-Deck Sound Operator is tracking down John the Baptist's microphone since he has been beheaded and no longer needs it. I am alone in the booth, making my way through a fistful of taffy, when another crew member enters who has a sweet tooth of her own. After we parse the colour difference between mango and apricot, I ask what she thinks of Barrett.

A conniption of anger ripples across her face, but she catches it. "I need this job," she says.

"It's okay," I tell her. "I will call you Deep Throat."

Deep Throat straightens her back. "Barrett is a fourteen-year-old."

I assume she is referencing the amount of hair gel he uses or the number of T-shirts he has with words on them, but she clarifies.

"He insists on getting his way, and when he doesn't, he sulks until he does. And look at who he's cast in lead female roles. They're skinny, young, and attractive, even when their husbands aren't."

I have been thinking this for a while but have lacked the courage to say it. Joanna, for example, is thin, blonde, and in her early twenties, while her husband, Chuza, is so middle-aged that his socks seem surgically attached to his upper calves. The other day, Litia pointed out Mother Mary's smokin' hotness, but upon seeing our geriatric Joseph, said, "I'd have remained a virgin, too." It is only Herodias, my wife, who is her husband's senior—just as Litia is to me.

Deep Throat tucks her tongue into her cheek and stares at me, appraisingly. "You Christian?"

Since all of the crew are paid, there is a higher percentage of non-religious people among them. Because of these odds, I gamble on honesty. "No."

"Me neither," she says, and together, in the darkness of the sound tech closet, we swear a heathen alliance. Through Deep Throat's headset, I hear the Stage Manager cue my entrance.

"Real quick," I say. "What happened to the old Martha of Bethany?"

Her eyes widen with fear. "What do you know?"

"I know nothing," I say. "I don't even know my lines."

She glances over her shoulder. "I'll tell you later."

"Heathen alliance," I whisper, holding out my fist.

"Heathen alliance," she whispers back, touching her knuckles to mine.

Onstage, Jesus enters my palace, but nobody much cares. I sashay around stage, in between the High Priest and his entourage, around Chuza, my long red kimono trailing behind me like a fox tail. Herod's Advisor once asked me what it's like to act alongside Jesus. I considered her question. "I'm not sure," I said. "I don't really pay attention to Him in that scene."

She tapped her nose. "Nobody does."

I spot various Villagers peeking out from backstage, against the explicit commands of the directorial team, wanting to witness my performance. Behind me, my Bannermen slacken the Wall as their focus drifts to me. I stand behind Christ and place both hands on His shoulders and shake Him like a baby, and I hear Temple Guard Captain giggle backstage at my unfettered insolence. I keep my blocking random, unpredictable. Sometimes I ruffle His hair, sometimes I pinch His nose. Tonight, in honour of Servant of the High Priest, I slap Him in the eye.

Over the past several weeks, my character has garnered more and more acclaim. After rehearsal, I am besieged by admirers. "You're extraordinary," says one of my attendants; "You're brilliant," says another; "You're a godsend," says Herod's Advisor, and everyone concurs with the assessment. Pilate says I am "a pleasure to watch." Chuza says it is an "honour" to share my stage. Jesus Understudy descends from his perch in the back row to charge towards the stage and declares, loud enough for everyone to hear, "Come for Jesus, stay for Herod!" I always respond with a humble thank-you, sometimes asking for the retrieval of a simple glass of soda since the dust is quite parching and my scenes quite long.

In the time between auditions and rehearsal, I often wondered what would happen to me during the play. The summer was a wide and white canvas, full of possibility: I might learn how to sing, I might start a fist fight with Gabriel, I might get Lyme disease and hallucinate a reunification with God. The only thing that was so outlandish I hadn't considered it was that I would be liked.

These transformations are so common in the Bible—the evolution from villain into hero, from mongrel into Messiah. But have I actually changed, or am I just playing the part?

"To what extent will you push this secularization?" I asked Barrett as we sat in the second row and watched sheep get sacrificed to the living God.

"Until it's good," he said. "Is the saviour of the play Gay Jesus? I don't think so." He shrugged. "But I could be wrong."

And verily, I want him to be wrong. Because I want to believe that Gay Jesus has already arrived. I don't mean in this season's Christ, but rather in the show's real saviour: me.

⚔ ⚔ ⚔ ⚔

After my scene with Jesus, I try to track down Deep Throat, but she's disappeared. Entering the backstage armoury, I run into Pilate so hard that my gold necklaces chime off his breastplate.

"Have you seen where Barrett has blocked the trial scene?" he asks, referring to Scene 33c: Jesus Returned to Pilot.

"No," I say. "Where?"

"He put me in the corner," he says, his voice pinched. "Where the latecomer seating is."

According to the company's weather policy, in the case of rain, "The performance is considered complete once Jesus has been sentenced by Pilate," meaning that any cancellation of the play after this scene will not result in a refund. Ergo, the scene of Pilate's condemnation of Christ needs not only to function as the incident that pushes the play into climax but also as a possible conclusion. Barrett's decision to have Scene 33c take place in the corner farthest from the audience and hemmed in by retaining walls on three sides therefore seems perplexing at best and personal at worst.

"Barrett is punishing me for being the only one to oppose him." His face reddens, the same colour as his cape. "When I was Pilate in

137

the Matthew script," he says, "I did the trial on the highest point of the set, and all the audience could see me and everyone loved it and it was called"—his throat snags—"Pilate's perch."

I want to hold him, then, beside the armoury, noxious with the smell of sweat and unfading tuna sandwich. I want to gather him in my arms and whisper sweet nothings to him the way Litia does me when I have twisted myself shrill at the world's grand injustices. But mostly, I want to thank him because his summer of anguish has unearthed a sympathy within me that I was unaware existed.

And then, in a voice so full of longing it hurts, he says, "I was a fucking awesome Pilate in the Matthew script."

"I know you were," I say, fully believing in what I do not know.

‹ SCENE 15 ›

The first time we are to crucify Christ, the forecast has been calling for clear skies and high temperatures until nightfall, but dark clouds now ambush the horizon. Since Jesus can't be lifted onto the cross if there's lightning or strong winds, the Stage Manager says we will skip the scene and head straight to the burial.

Even in the gales, I can hear the onlooking Villagers exhale with relief. There has been much talk about the inevitability of this day, and its prolonging is appreciated.

Centurion, who leads the Crucifixion, gathered us all last Sunday morning to tell us of his sorrow. "And my heart isn't in it," he said, eyes pink. "But the Lord needs my heart to be in it, so that is where my heart must be."

"Each year," said Capernaum Villager 1, "there is a small part of me that thinks maybe this season they'll cut it. But they never do."

"What did she think was going to happen?" I whispered to the dog. "A twist ending?"

But my glibness is only to mask fear. Consider, if you can, the deeper level of grief that awaits when you finally meet the man you have spent so long mourning only to kill Him again, like a marionette caught in a closed loop. I, too, sometimes feel that my actions are not mine alone, that they are directed by someone else, because who I am is not who I wanted to be, but to make any objection is to swim against the current. I once worked at a summer camp alongside a lifeguard who—like everyone else in her field—was half Confucian philosopher, half teenage fascist. "Every drowning," she would say to the campers as she walked the length of the dock like a drill master, "is because the person did not know themselves." In the Gospel of

Luke's later editions, Christ has a line added during the Crucifixion: "They know not what they do." But what if we know exactly what we're doing, and there's a certain safety in choosing which way the blood will spill? Consider, if you can, the unmitigated gall of He who preaches that we should plunge into fortunes unknown, and that our faith will keep us buoyant, when He can walk on water.

The storm descends, and everyone flees for shelter. The women use their headscarves to shield themselves from the wind as hail slices the air, ricocheting off Centurion's helmet. The Roman legion beats a hasty retreat, but Jesus is much quicker; wearing only a loincloth, He weaves between the armour-clad soldiers. Judas, Pilate, and I take shelter beneath the Temple arch.

Barrett, alone, remains onstage—his face (and hair) unyielding in the gusts.

"How old is he?" I ask.

"You'd have to check his manufacturing date," Judas says.

Over the course of the summer, there will be a suspicious number of storms that interrupt our rehearsal of Scene 36: The Crucifixion. The whole day will be arid right until Pilate hands Christ to the mob; suddenly, a bruised sky is upon us. I once pointed this out to Litia, mentioning that an inexplicable storm also happened during Christ's Crucifixion in the Gospels. She noted that the serendipity of these storms could be attributed to the fact that we always rehearsed the Crucifixion scene in the early evening, which is the most humid time of day and the period when most storms occur. I replied, "Right, that's what I'm saying," and she paid me the kindness of pretending to believe me.

There are, however, other parallels between a scene as it plays out during rehearsal and that same scene's depiction within the Bible. For example, we repeatedly rehearse the sheep-sacrificing scene, Scene 22b: Pilot Slays Galileans at Sacrifice; and even though the sheep are always terrified as they are led onstage to be sacrificed, bleating loudly, they somehow know to hush every time the Galilean gang slits their throats.

In a rehearsal of Scene 31: Peter's Denials, a seagull shrieks—multiple times—at the exact moment of the rooster's sound cue.

Most unsettling of all is one evening when we are running Scene 30: Jesus Betrayed/Arrested. In the Gospel of Mark, the arrest concludes with two verses about a nameless boy who was a follower of Christ; upon witnessing the Lord taken into custody, the boy panics, strips down, and flees naked into the night (Mark 14: 51-52). During our final run-through of the scene for the day, Maisy and I are backstage, eating a Villager's homemade jam, when we are interrupted by a teenage boy, half-dressed in an untied housecoat, a boy whom I have *never seen before nor will ever see again*, sprinting in a dead heat, screaming whether anyone has a plunger.

Fearing mockery, I tell Litia none of this.

Because of how much time the storm takes to pass, the Stage Manager announces that all actors not in the burial scene are released for the day.

"Lucky bastard," Pilate tells me, assuming I will head to the parking lot with Judas and the rest of the cast except for himself, Joseph of Arimathea, Gabriel, a couple of Roman soldiers, and the three Marys (Magdalene, the Virgin, and the Mother of James). Even Jesus gets to go.

But I am not done for the day. In addition to Herod and my small part in the genealogy sequence, I have been assigned a third and final role as Uriel, the archangel who joins Gabriel atop the empty tomb of Christ to greet the grieving women.

The hail lessens, but the rain continues to spit as we resume rehearsal. The Stage Manager comes across the loudspeaker: "Uriel to the tomb, please."

"When I'm an angel," I mumble to Pilate, "I get a *please.*"

The tomb is only accessible from onstage, and the directors don't want the audience to see me enter but rather want me to emerge mystically from within. They hatch a plan:

After Christ has been lowered from the cross and onto a waiting stretcher, His lifeless body is surrounded by a huddle of soldiers who camouflage Him in Roman red. He then rises, hidden within plain sight of the audience, and marches offstage. In His place, a mannequin (previously cached behind the cross on the right) is laid onto the stretcher and covered by a purple blanket. I, dressed as a Roman soldier, am one of the two stretcher-bearers who carries the Christ mannequin into the tomb, where I remain, performing my quick-change into the angelic uniform of rose gold and baby blue.

Uriel's costume is woven of flowing strips of fabric. Backstage and in broad daylight, the Head of Wardrobe always makes the change seem easy: "It's a tank top that goes to your ankles." But the grave is as dark and small as a grave. And in that tight space and time, I strip down to my boxers only to—try after try—get tangled to the point of bondage.

The process is made even trickier because, halfway through, the Virgin Mary and Mary Magdalene enter the tomb to weep over the body and further crowd an already itty-bitty space. All the while, as we run and rerun the scene and the cold rain continues to pour, the real Christ is backstage in a hot shower, washing the chocolate syrup blood off His chest and thighs.

Why is it so easy to mock faith and so hard to have it? Sometimes, when I am contorting into yogic poses to find my tank top's arm hole, I spot Mary Magdalene laying her shaking hands atop the mannequin's chest even though she knows the audience cannot see her, and I will be so physically and emotionally uncomfortable that I'll have to bite my lip to suppress a bout of church giggles.

Isn't the difference between beauty and bizarrity always a simple matter of distance? The brushstrokes of Mona Lisa's hair are over-worked and under-shaded; the feet of Rodin's *The Thinker* are webbed and gouty; Brando's Colonel Kurtz is more indigestion than genius: look at anything close enough—say, in some claustrophobic cave— and you see the faults. But what is far more striking than the flaws is the staunchness of faith despite them, the acknowledgement of something's imperfection while maintaining the belief that it is perfect.

Earlier that day, when the sun was blazing, I watched Jessica teach the mob to chant "Crucify." "It's three syllables," she said, "and I want you to enunciate each one: *kroo-see-fy.*"

The crowd started their chant, hesitant at first, but slowly gathering volume.

"Don't forget the fists," Jessica shouted, pumping her arm, and the crowd—one by one—raised their hands while tears streamed down their cheeks.

"*Kroo-see-fy.*"

"*Kroo-see-fy.*"

"*Kroo-see-fy.*"

During a brief pause for the On-Deck Sound Operator to adjust Pilate's microphone, I saw a senior Villager comfort a younger one. "We have to do this," she told him, holding his head against her neck. "I'm so sorry, but we have to."

Watching them, I felt the planet darken. But it was only the storm moving in.

Once the Marys have left, promising to return tomorrow, I have fifteen seconds to double-check my costume. But if I have been swift in my actions and Magdalene has been long in her lines, I am afforded a moment of stillness with the body of Christ. I listen to the rain against the roof, to the shale beneath my sandals, to my own softening breath. Once, in the half-light, I stared at the mannequin for so long I thought it moved.

"Are you ready?" I hear a voice say, and I do not know what to answer.

"Herod—I mean, Uriel," the Stage Manager repeats. "Are you ready?"

Through a hidden door in the rear of the tomb, I exit to where Gabriel is waiting. Together, we summit the burial mound, where I chastise the grieving women who, as promised, have returned the next day. "Why are you looking in the place of the dead for someone"—I pause, raising my hands like a maestro—"who is ALIIIIVE?"

"Cut," Barrett says. "You cannot say the line like that."

"I thought it played well," I say.

"No," Barrett says. "It didn't."

"Am I going to get wings too?" I say, pointing at Gabriel.

Behind us, the Stage Manager stifles a laugh. "We couldn't even afford one pair," she mumbles.

"Just say the line normally," Barrett says, then adding something he hasn't said all summer: "Please."

Pilate, despite being done for the day, has stayed to watch. He is sitting on his perch, rain drizzling down his face. He hears Barrett's final word, and he nods to me.

But what is normal for an angel? So I don't play Uriel like an angel at all. I play him like a man—a tetrarch, specifically. I play Uriel like he is Herod in disguise, having snuck into the tomb to have discovered whether Christ was charlatan or saviour. And then, after spending such a long night in the darkness, he exits the following morn to show comfort to his ramshackle subjects, bringing the solace that faith affords, proclaiming to the world that he has seen inside the tomb and Christ is not there. The eyes of the women light up with wonder, and I gaze into the empty audience—where the multitudes will watch—and I know their faces will shine with the selfsame comfort.

And so I, two thousand years in the future, give Herod what he has so long thirsted for: white robes, a trumpetous soundtrack, and the certainty the comes from having glimpsed the other side of the curtain.

When Gabriel and I exit, sometimes I try to hold his hand. Sometimes, he lets me.

‹ SCENE 16 ›

I catch a ride with Judas from the amphitheatre to the potluck. "We're into the single digits," he says, referencing the number of rehearsal hours we have before dress rehearsal.

"A lot can happen in a few days," I say. "Like the creation of the entire world."

"Have you *watched* the genealogy sequence?" he says, gripping and regripping the steering wheel.

We follow the line of other cars down the campground road, and our caravan kicks up a cloud of dirt. When we park, the dust settles, and the old Martha of Bethany is standing before us.

She is the only one clean in the filthy afternoon, her braided red hair glistening as the light sparkles in the large jar of sun tea she is holding. She seems a vision, and it is only when Judas jumps out of his car—the keys left dinging in the ignition—to hug her, that I realize she is real.

In the lineup for food, I give up my spot to Temple Guard 8 so I can stand beside her.

"You know," I say, taking a fistful of cherry tomatoes off the veggie platter, "the cast misses you terribly."

"Really?" she says, and her lips—remarkably unchapped—flex into a smile.

"How are you doing?"

She shrugs. "Good. Just kind of humiliated."

"You're humiliated here?" I say. "*Here?*"

As the summer continues and sleep deprivation sets in, most actors have become like kids at summer camp, applauding at any and all secrets shared. Grown men hug each other for such long periods of time that the first time I saw two Apostles do so, I thought they were Greek wrestling. This morning—just hours before—I spent a half-hour quietly crying in the amphitheatre's audience for no other reason than that I knew no one would mind.

"Yeah," the old Martha of Bethany says, brushing the hair from her face. "Here."

We reach the end of the line, and I look to the picnic area and see Simon Peter's Wife pointing at us while whispering to Diabolos.

"Why did you leave?" I ask the old Martha of Bethany.

She looks up from her paltry helping of potato chips and half-ladle of mac n' cheese with hot dogs. "You don't know?" she says, and I shake my head. "It was, um"—but then Diabolos is upon us.

"How you kids doing?"

"Fine," I say, and the old Martha of Bethany nods, eyes down.

"We've saved a spot for you over there," he tells her and points to where Simon Peter's Wife is waving.

The old Martha of Bethany files towards the picnic table. When she sits, Simon Peter's Wife wraps her arm around her and holds her close.

"We can make some room for you too," Diabolos says.

"No, that's okay," I say. But I can't find a spot anywhere else, so I sit on the steps to the bathroom, throwing cherry tomatoes in a high arc for the dog to pluck out of the sky.

⁂

Back at the amphitheatre, I tell Pontius Pilate and Jesus Understudy what happened at the potluck, how Diabolos and Simon Peter's Wife guarded the old Martha of Bethany, not letting anyone talk to her without supervision, until they escorted her to her car and she left.

"There's something you need to understand about this place," Pilate says. "Spiritual warfare has been a common occurrence around the Passion play since it started. The play is perceived as something that is doing God's work, and the Devil is trying to tear it down. Occasionally, things get in that don't have a place here, things that are not of God. That has happened this summer."

"Wait," I say. "What?"

"A girl I dated," Jesus Understudy says, "had a father who moved outside of town to get away from spirits. But spirits are not a thing for me."

"I wish I could say the same thing," Pilate says to him. "But I've seen shit that makes no fucking sense. I have participated in exorcisms that have been supported by the Passion play. I saw people come off the ground—and I'm not talking like they fucking jumped, I'm talking like they came off the ground for a sustained period of time."

"To me," Jesus Understudy says, "that means you were probably high."

"I was *not* under the influence of other substances," Pilate says. "I mean, at that point in my life, I did use a lot of substances, but I wasn't at that time."

The Playback Operator walks by, and we all shush. When we're alone, Pilate continues: "Is there spiritual warfare at the Passion play? Personally, I have seen things that lead me to believe that yes there is. Is the old Martha of Bethany a terrible person? No, the old Martha of Bethany is not a terrible person. The old Martha of Bethany is a wonderful person who I adore the shit out of."

"You're saying she was, like, possessed?"

"Last year," Jesus Understudy says, "when we were rehearsing, some guy came over the hills and yelled at me, 'You're part of the Illuminati!' And I danced at him. Because the Illuminati don't dance."

Pilate says, "I also believe in Sasquatches. I watched fucking *Harry and the Hendersons* when I was seven years old and it scared the everliving fuck out of me, and that's why I'm scared of Sasquatches to this day. And I place that in the same realm as spiritual warfare."

We are called to stage, which means it is time for Jesus Understudy to head to his exile in the upper audience.

"You know," Jesus Understudy says, staring at his sneakers, "I dated this other girl, who said, 'You realize you're actually somewhat attractive?' And I was like, 'You're wrong, but thank you.'"

Pilate rests his hand on Jesus Understudy's chest. "You better open your heart to this because this shit is going to hit home: I think you are by far the strongest, best Jesus actor I've worked with, and I've worked with fucking all of them. I loved every moment of watching you."

Jesus Understudy laughs. "Are you high?"

I turn to face him, narrowing my eyes, and with every fibre of my being, wish for the Lord—the real one—to strike him down.

⁂

The morning of our final run-through before dress rehearsal begins with a marvellous omen. I am inside the campground's food truck, preparing the dog's breakfast, when Diabolos asks me, "Did you hear the good news?"

I hesitate. "Like, God?"

"Baby's coming," he says, a quiver in his voice.

Our cast includes a soon-to-be-father Villager whose wife has been in her final trimester all summer. Diabolos tells me she went into labour late last night.

At the amphitheatre, I overhear the Stage Manager telling the directors that the soon-to-be-father won't be able to make rehearsal today. "Who is he?" Jessica asks.

"A nobody," the Stage Manager responds.

Backstage, everyone is getting into costume: cloaks are being wrapped, chain mail is shined and wings donned. I find Pilate and tell him about the soon-to-be-father and the imminent birth.

"That's nice," says Pilate, who is performing deep lunges in his thigh-high tunic.

"Has his wife ever been in the play?"

He uprights and buckles on his scabbard. "She was our Holy Spirit last year."

"Wait," I say. "There was a female Holy Spirit last year?"

He unsheathes his sword and nods.

"So this is the CBPP's *second* year of having a female Holy Spirit," I say, "but people are still pissed?"

Pilate laughs, flicks the sharpness of the blade. "I know, right?"

Once all actors are dressed, the first thing I notice is that the feet of the patriarchal cast members are like chicken claws in both thinness of toe and length of nail. I then see that Roman Servant 1 (a.k.a. Mulan) has been costumed in a red dress, thereby forcing her choice of performed gender. The third and final thing I note is the silence: everyone is flipping through their scripts. Even Woman (Scene 20) is going through her lines, despite Scene 20 being cut weeks ago.

Aside from me and Maisy, the only other person not checking their script is the Son of God. Instead, He is beside me, checking His hair in a backstage mirror, perfecting His bangs beneath His braided leather headband.

"The second I go bald," He says, "is the second I become a director."

I am unsure if He is speaking to me or His reflection.

"There's such stigma about aging in our field of work," He says.

I want Him to think that I, too, am enlightened, so I say, "I think women have it a lot worse."

"Totally," He says, smoothing His curls. "Sometimes I see a bald woman and I think, *Oh, man.*"

The Assistant Stage Manager calls places, and we scamper to await our entrances. Simon Peter is cued, walking onstage to drag his tangled fish nets while lamenting to the bluebird sky, "Empty nets, empty purse, whine-whine-whine."

The Assistant Stage Manager listens to her headset, nods, and says, "Go genealogy."

Jessica has simplified the genealogy sequence to the point that a sheepdog could lead it. However, this new, bare-bones choreography means that yet another version of instruction has been layered atop. Cain forgets his new blocking and prematurely shoves his brother, knocking free Abel's plastic torch, which smashes on the stones and sends D-size batteries rolling across the stage. Peleg is performing a four-week-old version and is the only one to thrust his golden sceptre into the air when Gabriel cries, "Israel!" Noah, running Friday's version, keeps walking towards the fire even though the lineup behind him has stopped, and thus appears to be an old man wandering forlorn and alone, looking for his grandchildren.

Our lines, too, are slipshod. The Holy Spirit interrupts Abraham's pleading with God, and — in the confusion — Isaac says, "Like the sands by the sea," instead of "Like the stars in the sky." Jacob, instead of running the heads-up play of switching his line with Isaac's, simply repeats his own. "Like the sands," he says, "still by the sea."

There is an upswing of energy during the birth of Christ, when the Angel Choir sings impeccably, but all momentum is halted upon the entrance of John the Baptist.

From the first day of rehearsal, John the Baptist has taken his epithet not in the first-century sense of someone who baptizes but rather in the twenty-first-century sense of Southern preacher. "The LoOoOord," he would croon to his congregation. This interpretation, however, was unwanted by the directorial team, and he was recently forced to undergo "character work" with Barrett. The result is evident within the first seconds of his entrance: John the Baptist — the wild man of the New Testament — has been lobotomized. "Come," he says. "Come," he says. "Come hear the word of the Lord," he says.

Every scene brings a fresh blunder. Simon Peter gets tangled in his fish net and trips out of the boat. The sound cue on Deaf Girl's healing is dropped, so it appears that Deaf Girl has not been healed at all. Chuza neglects to bring his stone tablet onstage and therefore reads Rome's morning declarations off the back of my grape bowl.

Even I can't keep it together. Instead of asking Jesus to make the Pharisees be quiet, I ask Him to make them disappear, a request considerably more difficult in live theatre. Then, in my tongue-tied distress, I demand that Jesus demonstrate His "pow-wow."

Maisy is the only one who nails it. She hits her marks, watches Pilate stutter and spit all over me, and then trots offstage.

Backstage, in the tomb of Christ, she is proud and panting. I frisbee my crown against the gate. "I'm sure it's real easy," I say, "when you don't fucking speak."

Intermission, and we break for potluck. At the campsite, we are stress-eating our way into third helpings when the soon-to-be-a-father arrives.

We watch him hop out of his truck and peruse the picnic tables, thrumming his fingers against his paper plate, before helping himself to a generous portion of Cheezies.

Officer of Herod asks, "Isn't your wife in labour?"

"Yeah," he says, slopping a pile of potato salad onto his plate, "but she's taking a really long time."

Man with Evil Spirit gasps. "Is she, like, okay?"

The soon-to-be-a-father nods but does not saying anything. He cannot say anything. For he has inserted an entire chicken wing into his mouth. And the bone is pulled out clean.

The second half of the show continues our train wreck. Dropped lines, dropped entrances, and, in the case of one Pharisee, a dropped ceremonial metal bowl which cling-clang-clongs down an entire flight of stairs. When Jesus is nailed to the cross, we are more relieved than anything.

Our dress rehearsal will be even worse. But we will push forth, through Gabriel's primary feathers getting snagged in the door hinge; through a Roman Soldier missing his entrance, leaving the Galilean rebel he is supposed to slay to fight to his own death against a ghost; and through the new ending that Barrett rewrote just hours before. Yet, in the midst of this theatrical triage, a far greater shortcoming will make itself known:

- "The owner will tell you upstairs—no, he will *take* you upstairs and tell you a large meal!"
- "I was born to speak the truth in the world, and about the world, and the truth, and those who speak to the world."
- "Father, forgive Me—I mean THEM. Forgive them…Father."

Our Lord and Saviour Jesus Christ does not know His lines.

But our run-through runs so long that our Lord has time to flip through His script before each entrance, and we remain unaware of what unfortunate future awaits.

It is dark by the time we gather around the campfire. Herod's Advisor cooks everyone s'mores while John the Apostle strums the introduction to "A Hole in the Bottom of the Sea." But by the way we sing about the flea on the tail on the frog on the who-the-fuck-cares, you can tell our hearts aren't in it.

Next morning, the soon-to-be-father's truck swerves down the dirt road. He hops out, and everyone gathers round.

His hair is greasy, and purple bags droop beneath each eye. His smile is so large it threatens to pop off his ears. "A girl," he says. "Sixty-nine pounds and twenty length in length."

Nobody bothers clarifying. We are overcome with joy.

‹ SCENE 17 ›

Days from opening, the work crew has hung a massive photo of the cast and crew by the front gate. In the photo's front row and on the very right, at the exact eye-level of all passing audience members, is Jesus Understudy. Everyone is in costume but him. He is wearing a bright blue dress shirt and is the only person kneeling on the shale. His hands are slack in front of him, and his face bears the expression of a hostage in an execution video: longing dulled by resignation.

Jesus Understudy walks up beside me, and peers at the photograph.

"I've been meaning to ask you," I say, "do you know what happened to the old Martha of Bethany?"

He glances at me and grins. "I can't comment."

"Why?"

"I can only tell you how I felt about it," he says, turning chipper.

"Okay. How do you feel about it?"

"I felt very uncomfortable because of what I saw."

"What did you see?"

In a sing-song, he says, "I'm not going to share that." He is so jovial that I begin to suspect that he doesn't know anything but is so desperate for human interaction that he is willing to string anyone along as long as they converse with him.

"What I saw doesn't make intellectual sense," he says, stroking his beard, "but it makes spiritual sense. So do you want my opinion or do you want the fact?"

"The fact."

"I can't tell the fact, but I can tell my opinion."

"Why can't you tell a fact?"

"Because I saw something that was more than fact."

"What did you see?"

"What I saw," he pauses, flashing his eyebrows, "is what I don't want to be the truth."

"I have no idea what you mean."

"I know," he says, rocking on his heels like a troll beneath a bridge. "You can ask questions and I can give answers, but I can't speak to a metaphysical experience."

"What did you see?"

"A metaphysical experience."

"Which manifested how?"

"As a metaphysical experience."

"Excuse me," I say. And I then say something that I know will wound him more than that crown of thorns ever did: "But I have a meeting with the real Jesus."

※ ※ ※ ※

The Dinosaur Hotel operates a walk-in closet from which they hawk off-sales. Litia has joined me for this ominous weekend, and we squeeze around flats of Coors Light and dusty two-litres of Coca-Cola. She discourages me from buying Bow Valley Lager, the cost of which flirts with the legal minimum. "You're drinking with *Jesus*," she says. "Shouldn't you be getting wine?"

"That means He'd be drinking His own blood," I say.

The bartender, who opened the off-sales closet for us, stands behind the register, picking her acrylic nails.

The six-pack rings through at six dollars even. I pass her a ten and ask if she's ever attended the Passion play.

"I keep meaning to," she says, handing me my change, "but I got beer to sell."

Outside, the marquee sign has more letters but makes less sense:

LIV EAM EV R Y WE

"What do you think it means?" I ask Litia.

"Live music every week?"

I shake my head and return to the car.

ппппп

The Lord's trailer boasts a 1970s extravagance: wood panelling, wallpapered roses, a frosted-glass decal. Acoustic music hums from His desktop computer as He welcomes me in, and I hand Him the beer.

"I have never heard of this brand," He says. "I'll put it in the minifridge."

Litia has stayed in the cafeteria to make year-end bracelets for her grade one class, and my hand twitches, searching for hers. In truth, I am scared of Jesus, but not because He is the lead. I am scared because I don't know what will slip out of my mouth when I am alone with Him; though, more to the point, I don't know what He'll say when He is with me.

The character of Christ has its own mythology, not just in the Bible but in the Badlands. The role has been known to — shall we say — change people. Take for example, the Jesus of seventeen years ago: Professional Model Jesus. With each of his four years as lead, he professed a deeper connection with the part, eventually believing himself to have acquired the facial features of Christ.[22] In his final year, a different gig forced him to cut his hair (à la Samson Agonistes); adamant that Jesus must have long locks, he purchased a sparse set of hair extensions, which dangled like thin braids (à la Alicia Keys), and no matter what the costume department said, he insisted on keeping them.

During that summer, he preached at a local church in Drumheller, and with his wife — the Oedipal Mother Mary — started a small ministry on the banks of the Red Deer River. "It was really fucking weird," Pilate told me. "And annoying. I'd known him for years and I still see

---

22 I have seen pictures. While he does bear a nominal resemblance to my Sunday school Jesuses, he has nothing on Jesus Understudy's separated-at-bris similarities.

him at auditions, and he has never been into method acting—before or since."

Furthermore, the husband-and-wife duo did all this despite Oedipal Mother Mary's struggle with alcohol that summer. According to Pilate, she wrapped her husband's Porsche around a lamppost late one night, and when the police arrived, she said her breath smelled of booze because she'd recently rinsed with mouthwash, and the cops *actually believed her*; both her survival of the wreck and the gullibility of the officers were taken by Professional Model Jesus as proof of God's favour for him and those he loved.

In Jesus' trailer, I point to a bookshelf. "Are these your books?"

He says they belong to His real-life wife, who has accompanied Him to Drumheller. He picks up Thomas Aquinas' *Selected Writings* and flips through the dog-eared pages. "I think she might've gotten Me this one." He tosses it back onto the shelf. "Haven't had time."

I don't realize how dry my tongue is until He offers me a beer and I accidentally chug it.

"Did you meet your wife in Vancouver?" I ask, swallowing a burp.

He nods. "I'd say it was a fluke, but I don't really believe in that." He pauses. "What do you believe?"

My cherished last lie; the very occasion for which I have kept it. All I need is to say, "I believe," and see myself saved.

But would you believe me, dear reader, if I told you my throat would not let the words escape?

The Lord sees straight through me. "Not everyone here is a believer." He takes a sip of beer and puckers at the taste. "A Christian doesn't feel they're religious. I mean, I guess technically we do religious practices because we pray. But to a Christian, it's just like, I'm not being religious, I'm just worshipping the living God."

I ask Him why He never attends Sunday Worship at the campground.

"I don't know where the campground is," He says.

I explain to Him the turnoff. "It's right before the dinosaur statue," I say. "But I suppose that doesn't really narrow it down." I start describing other landmarks, the abandoned coal mining carts and the ATV parking lot, but I see His gaze drift into another world. He has no plans of visiting; the man is Christ, for Christ's sake. The financial future of the country's largest stage rests squarely on His shoulders. How could that not swagger His step? The play has turned His life into a diamond: all the beauty, all the pressure.

The Lord stands to get us another beer. On His table lies this year's freshly printed program. The cover photo of Christ is not our Jesus, or even last year's, but is rather the Best Jesus Ever. I flip through and see that not only are typos rife throughout, but there is also a full-page Travel Drumheller advertisement of the Best Jesus Ever releasing a dove. Our season's Jesus has been relegated to a toonie-sized headshot on the penultimate page with a bio shorter than the Intern Director's.

As He pops both beer tabs, the screen door wheezes open, and Jesus' real-life wife enters and introduces me to her friend Kyla.

"Are you having a little interview hang-out time?" Jesus' real-life wife asks. She looks to Kyla. "He's Herod," she whispers.

"Yes," I say. "I am."

Jesus' real-life wife and Kyla sit on the couch near us, and I ask Jesus why He thinks anyone would volunteer here if they're not religious.

"People come for all reasons," He says. "This one couple told Me, 'If we're part of the Passion play we have a free place to park our camper.'"

I am fairly confident that this is Cleopas and his real-life wife, who runs the gift shop. They're the only ones at the campground who own an RV.

"But there must be something else," Jesus adds, extending a long finger towards me. "Something tugging at the heart."

Cleopas is also the one who bugles us to prayer each Sunday morning.

I ask, "Do you need to believe in Christ in order to be Him?"

He says maybe a non-Christian could do it, but there is a depth you descend to when your life eclipses the Lord's. "Like today," He says, "during the rehearsal of the Crucifixion, I missed the sandpit, and I fell right on the gravel. And it hurt, but I kept going. Like a champ."

"He had a graphic Band-Aid," Jesus' real-life wife adds.

"Mickey Mouse," He nods.

She says, "God is like, 'You want to live out My purpose, then live out Me.'" She looks at her husband. "I've bought Him two books, and they have been books that He's read and have contributed to His understanding of Christ's character."

Long before I started this summer, before I descended into the Badlands, even before I opened the email that said I was crowned tetrarch, I had decided to hate Jesus. No matter how charming or humble or brilliant He was, I was going to find some seam within Him and rip it open.

The greatest kindness that God affords is His ability to act as the customer complaint box on all matters. And I need someone to blame for the worst parts of myself, the parts I know best: my childish compulsion to create evil within Eden, to spurn what I crave, to mock what I admire. Such a thrill I get in outfoxing the unwary. I had decided to hate Jesus because of whom He's related to, because of my belief that the faults of my character rest not with me but with the playwright. But this offloading only works if you believe that a Creator exists. Without God, there is only accountability.

Since arriving at the Passion play and spending so much time with those who wring glee from the simplest moments, I've had to confess how much of my own day I spend being sad. I have long suspected this but have never had to admit it until I sat beside Grumbly Pharisee on the tailgate of his half-ton as his jaw literally dropped at the Holy Spirit pirouetting on repeat in the centre of the campground's field, earbuds in, Her planted foot spinning up the pollen. Sunday mornings have become especially hard: an hour before Worship, where we all beg fate to be kind with our lamb-skinned lives, I take the dog to the riverbank and stand in the floodplain. A duck bobs in the ebb; a murmur of sparrows shape-shifts above the aspens; a motorcyclist on the far side of the water rides without a helmet, and her long black hair banners behind. All the while, I am holding court in my skull-sized kingdom, shuttered to the world. A man I once loved said, "Let the dead bury the dead," and I fear this is the future for me: some immortal inability to accept joy.

Jesus and I drink late into evening. I offer the two remaining cans of beer to Christ's real-life wife and her friend Kyla, but they examine the label and say they've got wine. The Lord concludes His point about how people who object to the apocryphal liberties taken with the script (Herod playing bocce ball with a dog, for example) are the equivalent of people who say, "The movie wasn't as good as the book." The four of us laugh so hard that my laugh turns into a burp, which makes us laugh even harder. Behind Jesus, through the window halo-ing His head, the green leaves of poplars applaud in the breeze.

Jesus' real-life wife says that if she were speaking to those who took issues with the theatricality of the script, she would say, "There's going to be somebody who is like Herod, and that person needs to see themselves onstage. They will not relate to an Apostle. They will not relate to the Thieves on the Cross. We need to have that person see Herod and go, 'Shoot, that's me.'"

"Shoot," I say.

"Even Herod," she says, "had an aspect of him that the Lord wanted."

Suddenly, it is all too much. The evening light, the cheap beer, the breeze through the screen door; and then, too, there is Jesus, His real-life wife, and her friend Kyla, all within arm's reach. To not just glance at grace but to sit across the table from it and have it crack you a cold one—after that, what is left to live for?

In my throat, I get the same eye-watering welt as if I'd taken a shot of tequila—and I am hit with that rush of adrenalin paired with the creeping sense that what is about to happen is beyond my control. "I need to leave," I say, and they all insist we do this again, but I know we never will.

In the cafeteria, Litia is braiding her bracelets. "How'd it go?" she asks, packing her threads.

Before this project, I was worried that there wouldn't be enough to write about. But how to explain that I am now worried there is far too much, that I am stricken with doubt, and that my heart is breaking but I'm not sure why? So all I say is, "Everything's fucked," and she nods as if she understands.

On the long drive to Calgary, I look at her whenever we pass an oncoming car, hi-beams brushing her face. I want to offer her the Promised Land, legions of sunburnt slaves kissing her feet, but all I've achieved is ordering my umbrella bearer to fetch her an iced tea, and by the time the paper cup was carried across the parking lot, the drink was no longer iced.

Whatever we worship, we do so solely for the reason it is not us. The moments I feel the closest to Litia are the ones I feel the most alone, when I feel that no matter how tightly I cling to her, she remains separate from me. At the end of each day, we all must sleep in our own bodies.

"Oh, no!" Litia shouts. Out the windshield, the headlights touch the white stripe of skunk before it disappears beneath the undercarriage.

"No no no," she says, pulling the vehicle onto the shoulder and resting her forehead against the steering wheel. "What do we do?"

"We have to go back," I say.

"To see if he got away?"

"To see if we have to kill it."

She hangs a U-ey, but the asphalt's clean. We troll the shoulder to see if the wheels threw it into the ditch but don't see anything.

"We passed over him," Litia says. "A miracle."

And I believe her. I do. Until hours later, when we arrive at our apartment, and I open the passenger door to the smell, pungent as sin. We have been dragging him for the entire ride home.

ACT III:

PERFORMANCE

‹ SCENE 1 ›

Between the end of rehearsals and the beginning of performances, something odd happens: I become friends with the cast. Odd, in that I finally admitted it to myself. Because with every inning of slow-pitch softball, every Israeli-themed breakfast, every hand-held leap into the river, I became more and more myself, only to find myself more and more accepted. Mary Mother of James checks out my poetry collection from her community library. Lead Drummer buys a book on common mispronunciations, solely to invite me over to his trailer, where we eat homemade muffins and marvel at the fact that *sherbet* has only one *r*. Baptizee 4 lauds my potluck contributions as expanding the culinary horizons of the cast with the "exotic spices" of cumin and celery seeds.

And how deeply I regret my lies to Diabolos and Simon Peter's Wife, saying I was something I was not. With Diabolos in particular, I have become so overwhelmed with the desire to confess that I often need to leave our lunch table or fake an emergency phone call while we sing "This Little Light of Mine" at the campfire. Sometimes, I pretend to be asleep during our carpool, as he notes the play of the evening light on the homesteads, knowing that if I spoke, my next words would be, "I'm sorry." But how could I ask for forgiveness? I lied about the one thing you cannot lie about. And so, in my own cowardice, I convince myself that he somehow knows, but of course this is just another lie.

Like me, Litia, too, has grown fond of the cast. Last week, Herodias waved at her from across the cafeteria, saying, "I saved a spot for you," then shooing Fisherman 2 away. Unlike me, however, Litia has not spun a summer's worth of deception that she is now cobwebbed into and cannot conceive a way out of.

"Do you feel bad about lying to them?" she asks me, as we take the dog for an early-morning walk by the river. The current is sluggish with July's crawling heat, and the reflection of the sunrise turns the water into a crimson wound, oozing from the centre of the earth.

"I'm not deceiving them any more than they're already deceived," I say, not entirely sure what I mean.

Because how am I to explain that what started out as a small untruth—as tiny as a mustard seed—has, over the course of a single summer, grown to such proportions that it now stands impenetrable between me and them? But to cut it down runs too high a risk. It would be like living in a treeless field, where every person can see everything about you. And what if they don't like what they notice? Or what if they don't notice anything, just a reedy little man being blown over by the rough wind of the world?

Four hours before the call for our first show, I am sitting on a picnic bench and waiting for Joseph of Arimathea and his real-life son, Adam, to get a game of frisbee going. As Adam corrals his friends (some Dark Angels, Roman Soldiers, and Demon Possessed Boy), I think back to when Simon Peter's Wife asked me if I was a believer. At the time, I told myself that in allowing Simon Peter's Wife to think I was like her, I would uncover a culture that has burrowed itself from the light and emerges only in the most staged instances. But I now admit that the real reason I lied was not to avoid the truth but rather to create it. When I told Simon Peter's Wife I was a believer, it was not because I was pretending to be one but because I wanted to be one, and in her question she unwittingly gave me the permission to do so. "Yes," I said, and knowing that there was no one to disprove me, the lie turned true.

***

Backstage is so silent you could hear a snake slither across gravel. Everyone is double-checking their costumes: straightening their robes, unwrapping and rewrapping their headscarves, tightening their sandals. The Dark Angels are finding the armholes in their perforated smocks while the Angel Choir coordinates the folds of their tulle gowns so their pink and blue stripes fall along the same parallel lines. Andrew the Apostle is standing board-straight, facing a retaining wall, with his forehead pressed against the cool concrete.

During the run-throughs and dress rehearsal, I allowed Maisy to mingle with everyone as they got ready, but today she can sense the tension and retreats into her tomb. I join her and begin to change into my costume. Through the synthetic rock, I hear the pilgrimaging hoards rumble into the amphitheatre.

I twist my rings on when the Assistant Stage Manager announces it's forty-five minutes until start. I don my necklaces: thirty minutes. I wriggle into my beige dress: ten minutes. I cover it all with my genealogy sequence's nondescript shepherding cloak, and we are being called to places.

Standing ready for my Temple arch entrance, I peer into the sixteen-year-old eyes of the Holy Spirit. They are pure fire.

"Go genealogy."

The audience is an ocean of Hawaiian shirts and pastel blouses. The men wear wide-brimmed safari hats while the women wear green-tinted visors.

But no one is watching us.

The Friday afternoon's apocalyptic temperature has afforded us a diversion. In the heat, audience members are falling like stone statues.

One of them face-plants hard in the aisle, and volunteer stretcher-bearers swoop in like Valkyries to ferry her away. A front-row patron keels forward off his seat, so nobody much notices that Noah arrives five beats early, or that Salah for some bewildering reason holds his sceptre like a hockey stick, or even that Enos accidentally pronounces his name "Anus."

Backstage, I tell Chuza about the size of the audience. "It's like a small city out there!"

But Pilate interrupts. "Vance spaces them out," he says. "He tells the ushers to leave empty seats between each person." He peeks around the stage left entrance. "We're not even half-full."

"Better than being half-empty," I say.

"No," he says. "If we were half-empty, we would have *more* people."

After the Angel Choir finishes their song and Mother Mary has groaned her way through labour, Herod et al. are cued to enter.

The audience, having been culled of the dead and dying, is now rapt in attention. They fan themselves with the aquamarine program and appear as a wall of ocean closing in.

I hop into the baptismal pond, and the cold water shocks the air out of my lungs.

It is my turn to speak, but all I can hear is the voice of the Devil in my heart: *Roles come to those who need them.*

Faith without a crisis is only credulity. Jesus Understudy once told me, "I firmly believe that people who believe in God are stupid. And I say that believing in God myself." He then got me to pay for his two beers and left, and the waitress came by and asked me if I wanted anything, and I answered but had to repeat myself because the first time was nothing more than a whisper.

All I want is to believe in God.

In the baptismal pond, I have forgotten my line. But I am not worried. I do the trick I taught myself during dress rehearsal: I become very still and focus on the soft heat of my mic pack, which—because of all the time I spend splashing around in water—I don't wear in a belt beneath my costume like the rest of the actors but in a shoulder harness, the pack double-bagged by two black condoms and tucked between my shoulder blades; and I focus on that spot—halfway between my head and my heart—and speak whatever words come to me, and trust that they are close enough.

※ ※ ※ ※

Intermission takes place at dinnertime. Backstage, some cast members unpack three-course meals, replete with cutlery, bottled drinks, and dipping sauce. Other actors get the concession's leftover hot dogs, but there are no vegetarian options.

Noah saunters by, and I jog to catch up with him.

"What can I do for ya?" he says.

"You told me a little while ago about the"—I lean in—"miraculous events that take place here. Can you tell me more?"

His meringue eyebrows furrow as his black eyes search my face.

"Alright," he says, and waits while I find a blank page in my notebook. "Do you want an old one or a new one?"

"The best one," I say.

"Indeed."

I am expecting the deaf to hear and the blind to see. I am expecting the tremors of a Parkinson's patient to halt. Clouds parting, the sun cathedralling through, and a dove taking flight from within a patron's cowboy hat. At the very least, orthopaedics will be left in the aisle.

Instead, the story can be summed up as follows:

A non-religious woman saw the show and enjoyed it.

"And?" I say.

"And," he says, smiling. "I *think* Diabolos might know her husband or brother or something." He puts his hand on my pen, which has yet to start writing. "But don't quote me on that."

That's it. That is the miracle.

It is not that he has disappointed me but rather that he has lived up to my expectations, joining the ranks of every other big-city charlatan, promising wonder and delivering let-downs.

"If you'll excuse me," Noah says, "I've got a hot dog to eat."

I am starving and resentful, so I eat the bread of the Last Supper. I leave the crust intact but tunnel into the cleaved loaf, scooping out ice-cream balls of dough. My umbrella carrier catches me. Mouth full, I ask, "You got a problem?"

She rolls her eyes and walks away.

The second act begins, and it is time for Maisy to make her entrance. I retrieve her from the tomb, and we position ourselves in the middle of our entourage, behind the stage-right gates. The Assistant Stage Manager holds up her hand to count down.

Five.

Four.

I touch my forehead to Maisy's. "Whatever happens, as long as we don't bite anyone, they can't touch us."

Two.

The gates swing open, and a thousand necks crane our way. From the audience a man, his voice bubbling with Albertan twang, says — clear as a bell — "Oh my golly, that be a doggy!"

I am ready, then, for Maisy to bolt, for her to find the man, and for the two of them to howl with happiness together. But she only turns to Wealthy Herod Guest 3 and begs out a treat. Pilate enters and screams at me for a bit, glancing at Maisy, who yawns dramatically and lays down, her chin resting on the Temple steps.

On our exit, she trots beside me. "A miracle," I say to her.

She stops in her tracks and turns her head. "Yes," she says. "I am."

The show receives a standing ovation, but Judas tells me that always happens. "What are they going to do? Stay seated?"

After the bow, Pilate and I change out of Galilean garb and into our real costumes. When we re-enter the stage, a Disneyland-length line is waiting for us. At first, I am unsure how to act, but I come to see that everyone is so enamoured with me that I can act however I want. When people want a picture, I begin dressing them up in various parts of my costume: my chiffon sash, my numerous necklaces, my large red kimono. "Who wants the crown?" I say to a group of three women, holding it high above them, and when they all reach for it, I see that each of them has prosthetic arms. And as I wedge the crown in between one women's plastic fingers, I grow briefly yet tremendously sad, knowing this is the happiest I will ever be.

Jesus Understudy has watched the show from the tech booth with his girlfriend, Head of Sound. He takes the centre aisle's steps two by two to budge my lineup, all to point across the stage at Christ, who is checking His phone. "Nobody's visiting Him," Jesus Understudy says—then, looking over his shoulder and a bit louder: "Nobody!"

My lineup continues to grow, and people start budging to join the photos of strangers.

"We're all believers here," one father says to his daughter as she sheepishly stands beside two elderly women. "Now squeeze in, sweetheart."

A group of six Spanish-speaking women—all of them wearing the same tour group T-shirt—make a photograph sign with their hands. They giggle coquettishly, and I am so proud that I exclaim the only Spanish I know: "Tengo hambre," which means "I'm hungry"—except, as I realize much later, I mess up the pronunciation and say "Tango hombre," which loosely translates into "dance, man." The women all look up at me, quizzically, and then begin to dance, hesitant and wooden but still grooving, and I—no longer having any idea what is happening—do so with them. The setting sun catches my jewelry as I swirl, scintillating, like a first-century disco ball.

Some people don't want or say anything. They simply place their blue-veined hands on my forearm. One woman, her eyes raw with tears, takes my hand and presses both her thumbs into my palm. "I know," I say to her, "I know." But what it is I know, I do not know.

In the coming shows, these lineups will only continue to grow, snaking up the aisles into the amphitheatre's second tier. Sometimes, Pontius Pilate (whose lineup also spans postal codes) will march his legionnaires my way, and together we will improvise small scenes. Pilate, defying the Stage Manager's clear and repeated instructions, will unsheathe his sword and perform various tricks, twirling it through the air and slashing it at me.

Our most beloved skit is when Pilate takes a boy from the lineup and commands his soldiers to execute the child. I intervene on the boy's behalf. "You can't decapitate him," I say, placing my crown atop his head, "because he is a king!"

"Tetrarch," Pilate corrects, shoving the dimple-cheeked child back to his mother, who is filming it all on her phone. Pilate then leads his soldiers to patrol the upper exit, and the boy's mother continues to film him the entire time he walks away.

Then, too, is the jaw-dropping number of people I know: family acquaintances, fellow writers, the ex-girlfriend of my best friend. One night I greet a friend of my father's whom I haven't seen for twenty years. "I didn't know you'd be in the play," he says, and I reply, "I didn't know you'd be in the audience."

But despite these hordes, nobody ever asks me about Herod's theology, and I will never get the chance to say the monologue that I have been practising every morning for the past week: that there seems to be something fundamentally unfair about faith, that those who need it the least, like the Apostles, get to witness all the miracles they desire, but those who need it most are met with only with silence. I peek over at Judas, who is often surrounded by a handful of audience members. "It's hard," I hear him say, "but I think he did it because he believed so much in what he was doing. And does that make it wrong?"

⁜⁜⁜⁜⁜

The opening-night cast party takes place beside the amphitheatre, beneath a bigtop tent. Vance has set up a buffet, and there are so many vegetarian burger patties that I stack two triple-deckers, but the metal tray remains overflowing. "You'll come back, right?" he says.

I agree, but as I walk away, I'm not sure what I have agreed to.

Now that the play has opened, all conversation has turned to who is returning next season.

Among the crowd, I track down Deep Throat, my counterpart in the heathen alliance. She is by herself at a table, nibbling her way through a handful of carrot sticks.

"Okay," I say, sitting down across from her. "What happened to the old Martha of Bethany?"

She picks at her food and explains to me that the old Martha of Bethany hears voices. Like many people with this illness, these voices are exacerbated by stress. During the first week of rehearsal, she suffered an episode in the middle of the amphitheatre. In response, Simon Peter's Wife whisked the old Martha of Bethany away into a tiny room, where Simon Peter's Wife attempted an exorcism on her, the effect of which was the frenzying of an already frantic situation. All the while, the Holy Spirit wandered the stage, wondering where Her sister went.

Soon after, the play's leadership kicked old Martha of Bethany out of the play. For our second week of shows, she will volunteer in the parking lot, semaphoring RVs into stalls.

Deep Throat looks up at me. Water tension holds the tears from falling off her eyelids. "They made the decision while we were rehearsing the healing of the Man with Evil Spirit."

Stories in the Bible never turn out the way you think they will. The Scriptures hardly ever have a coherent theme, let alone moral—and in that sense are unexpectedly true to life: Jacob, after decades of deception and polygamy, eats his just deserts by siring all of Israel; the ark finally runs aground only for Noah to get drunk and naked in front of his kids; Jonah is burped out of the whale but then falls victim to heatstroke while cowering beneath a withered shrub.

I wanted my story of the CBPP to end the way the Bible should have: not with revelations of eternal suffering but with a group hug, a camp-wide song of "Ode to Joy" as together we ascend. I had wanted this so badly that backstage, while Simon Peter forsook Christ for the third time, I wrote the book's final paragraphs as a kind of prayer. But now, I look around at our cast and feel disgust to the point of pity. Our wish to be transported back to the yesteryears of olde—when Messiahs walked among us—has come true, and we have been pulled into a much larger story, one of Biblical proportions, a story of the saved and the forsaken, of great distances and inhuman heat, of spectacle and extinction, of deceit and madness, of power and fear.

I shove aside my plate and rest my forehead on the table. When I look up, Deep Throat has left. Grass fires have been engulfing the province. Baptizee 4 called it a "sure sign of the end of times." A westward wind surges into the tent and brings an ash so fine you could wash your hands with it.

‹ SCENE 2 ›

Near the end of grade nine, Father Bill summoned us for a meeting about Mel Gibson's recently released film, *The Passion of the Christ*. We were in science class, learning about the toxins produced from Alberta's coal plants, when we were told to cut the lesson short.

Jason D'Souza and I had seen the movie that weekend because it was rated R for violence and, more importantly, sex and nudity. But there was no sex, and the nudity turned out to be only a shot of Jesus' side-bum as He walked arisen from His tomb. Aside from one scene in which Jesus claims to have invented dining room furniture (which I only remember because I told my father about it, assuming that he—a cabinet maker—would appreciate the history lesson), the movie didn't really do much for me. Jason, however, became gleeful every time Christ was whipped, shouting in the packed theatre, "Drive that sleigh!"

Father Bill, who hated everything pop culture, surprised us. "The music, the acting, the cinematography," he said. "It'll be a crime if it doesn't win this year's Oscar."

Even more tragic than the fact he thought there was only one Oscar, this is the only time I can remember him happy. Pope Jean Paul II, whose picture hung above our school's fire exit, had been recently rumoured to have viewed the movie, saying, "It is as it was."

"And of course I agree with him," Father Bill said. "Mind you, it is still Hollywood. They went a bit overboard on the gore. It would have been medically impossible for Christ to have been beaten that badly and still carry the cross."

"Medically impossible?" Jason said. "Have you heard of the virgin birth?"

He was told to sit outside, and the banishment hit him like a lash.

"I fucking hate this," he said, the corners of his lips quivering. And in that moment, I saw he was not saying these things out of vengeance or malice or even to extend his tenure as class clown, but rather to simply understand why we believe what we say we believe. As I turned my knees to let him file from the pew, I imagined the lion-hearted bravery of standing up and saying the same. I rose, and Father Bill raised an eyebrow.

"Yes?"

Above me, the ceiling fans whipped with fury. And I peered down on myself from a great distance to hear me speak the words, "May I go to the washroom?"

"No," Father Bill said, and I retook my seat.

Jason and I stopped talking when he went to Catholic high school and I went to public. But our falling out wasn't for any religious reasons. At the time, I don't think there was anything we cared less about than God. Rather, he got into drugs and girls, and I got into turtlenecks and modernist poetry.

When I first arrived at Central Memorial High School, I spent the first month asking my new classmates which religion they were. Many were Christian, but some were atheists or Muslims or Hindus. One boy said he was Wiccan, and had the mascara to prove it. Though most exotic yet were the multitudes who answered, "I dunno."

Eventually, I realized my inquisition was putting people on edge and adopted a "don't ask, don't tell" policy. When I went to Saturday sleepovers, I'd bring a backpack of my next day's clothes—black jeans and a turtleneck. But tucked beneath those clothes were more clothes: a collared shirt and slacks, just in case we were to go to church the following morning, as I would with Jason and his family. I never used my formal wear, and when I finally took the clothes out of my backpack to make room for a bottle of pineapple liqueur, I saw that a leaky pen had tie-dyed the shirt with black flowers.

In drama class, I befriended a boy named Alex. We went to a community theatre's production of *Seussical*, after which he drove us to an all-night diner that still allowed smoking, where we ordered black coffee and no food. I forget what we talked about but I remember we did so until the ashtray was heaped, our eyes shot through with smoke, our hearts bucking with caffeine, nicotine, and the inexplicable knowing that our lives had started without us and we were already behind.

There is something unique about a best friend when you are a boy in the long bend of becoming a man, a camaraderie against the world you will one day inherit. It is an age of contradiction: conviction without experience, sexual desire without sexual understanding, an awareness of cruelty without any ability to stop committing it.

One night, alone in his '84 Land Cruiser—the dashboard stacked with fast food wrappers, our seats reclined, and cigarette smoke curling out the cracked window—I said, "Alex, I want to ask you something, but I don't want you to tell anyone."

He turned onto his side, the streetlamp spotlighting half his face. But before he could respond, I said, "What religion are you?"

Alex, lo and behold, was Catholic—had come from St. James School and switched into the public stream for the same fine-arts reason I had.

When are you who you truly are? When you're young and unsullied, believing what you dare to believe? Or when you have grown older and have become so nauseated by the hypocrisy of belief that you decide the only way to be genuine is to not have faith in anything?

That night, we fell asleep in the Land Cruiser. And I awoke not knowing where or who I was.

‹ SCENE 3 ›

Sunday afternoon, and I've swung open the TrailBlazer's back hatch. In the square of shade, Maisy and I are sitting on the bumper, sharing a tomato.

The new-father Villager drives by in his truck. Ever since his wife gave birth a week ago, he now takes any opportunity to bum around the campground, performing odd chores, inviting people to go tubing down the river, anything to hide from his future. John the Baptist stops throwing the football with Simon the Zealot to holler, "Go back to your wife and child!"

Like a cockroach when the light flicks on, the truck pivots and disappears. Its tires spin up dust, which the sun turns into long beams that reach from the Heavens through the canopy to shine like spotlights upon cast members as we revel in our scarce hours of free time: Temple Guard 6 practising her baton; a Dark Angel in a hammock, yawning like a cat, his tongue curling out; John the Baptist throwing a Hail Mary to Simon the Zealot. All of us becoming the stars of our own storylines.

As Maisy and I marvel at a rotating ray of light that follows Doubting Thomas as he whistles his way to the showers, Simon Peter hops onto the TrailBlazer's bumper, uninvited. Everything about him is large: his hands, his beard, the 1970s camper van that he sleeps in, equipped with tasselled curtains on each window. Even his to-go cup of black tea is the size of a wishing well's bucket. His judgement, too, is enormous. In this life, he brings large bags of candy to dole out only to those he finds worthy; in the next, he decides which lever to pull — the one that opens the pearly gates or the trapdoor. I notify him about his job as Heaven's bouncer, but he says he'd never thought about it.

"But I have family members," he says, "and I literally have the key to unlock their prisons, but they won't take it because every time I get close to them, I'm just that religious self-righteous guy."

He flicks a watermelon seed off his callused hands. "That is what we're doing here. People are in prison."

To be fair, the man does know something about personal prisons.

"I'm a former drug addict, adulterer, alcoholic," he says.

I hadn't known this for sure, but the amount of candy he ingests led me to certain assumptions.

"This past week," he continues, "my wife has been away, and I have been faced with ample opportunity to use and partake in every single temptation."

I glance around the campground. Every single temptation? Capernaum Villager 2 stands beneath a tree, wearing a straw hat and practising her violin for next week's Worship. A nearby Villager hums along as he chops some firewood. And because Pilate stays in town with his parents, and because Judas has become the Howard Hughes of the campground and no longer leaves his trailer, yesterday I finally cajoled Mary of Bethany and her real-life husband, Temple Guard 4, to share a bottle of wine with me; but even then, they insisted we drink out of coffee mugs, over which Temple Guard 4 would rest his hand whenever somebody walked by on the way to brush their teeth.

"And I haven't walked that journey perfectly," Simon Peter says. "There have been moments where I realize that nobody's watching. I can do *the thing* and chances are nobody's ever going to find out."

The more Simon Peter talks, the more the campground glistens with lust. By the picnic tables, Baptizee 4 whispers to Herod Attendant 2, lips mere millimetres from earlobe. Two women from the Angel Choir share a can of Mountain Dew. Capernaum Villager 2 vibratos her hand along the violin's fingerboard. A place which once seemed Edenic now seems so sinful, which — I suppose — makes it Edenic all the more. Why *does* his camper van need those tasselled curtains?

"But," he says, "I would literally get zapped by the Holy Spirit and be able to speak life to this other person."

"Do you believe in Hell?" I ask.

"I see people in Hell every day. I see Christians in Hell. And so was I. Man, I loved drugs. Especially coke."

I nod.

"Wow," he says.

I nod.

"Loved it," he says.

I nod.

"So good!" he says.

Current Events Villager peeks at us from between the poplar leaves. We make eye contact, and she pretends to be watching a squirrel.

"But eventually," Simon Peter continues, "the dark roots of those choices start to manifest themselves in a way that they became a burden, to a point where they don't work anymore."

The new-father Villager has returned, this time with inner tubes in his flatbed. John the Baptist has retired for a siesta, and the new father slows his truck as he rolls past the Baptist's site.

Last week, while Chuza and I chatted about literature, the new-father Villager joined our table. "Are you going to read to your baby?" Chuza asked him.

"Haven't thought about it," he replied. "But he sure is growing fast."

"*She*," Chuza said. "Your child is a girl."

"I know, I know," the Villager said. "But it's only, like, a week old, so give me some time."

"*She*," Chuza said. "*She* is only a week old."

Simon Peter and I watch the truck crawl along the road before Grumbly Pharisee, the new-father Villager's real-life uncle, chases it off-site, herding his nephew back to his life. Even after he gives hot pursuit, the greased black hair of Grumbly Pharisee—who resembles a chubby Rasputin—does not lose its centre part. He stops by the TrailBlazer as I ask Simon Peter about his political leanings.

Instead of talking about taxes or elections or even potholes,[23] he takes the question in an unexpected direction: "The most incredible church that did the most incredible work existed under Nero," he says, referencing the tyrannical and mutton-chopped emperor with an insatiable appetite for executing Christians.

"Interesting," Grumbly Pharisee observes, fingers stroking his coal-coloured beard. "Interesting."

"My friends are going to think I'm crazy for saying this," Simon Peter says, "but we would be better Christians if the vote was taken away from us."

"Wait," I say. "What?"

"If we didn't have the privilege to vote then we could concentrate on Jesus. That's what they did under Nero. Look at the persecuted Church where it is illegal to be a Christian and where they get killed. It is refined and pure."

"That is true," Grumbly Pharisee says. "That is true."

Simon Peter fidgets with the rim of his coffee cup. "I saw one of the church leaders from China visit North America, and he said that what we face here is harder because in China everything is so clear cut. But here"—he wedges the cup into the bumper's plastic joint and fixes his eyes on me—"you don't know who your enemy is."

Here is my chance—to undo what I should never have done, to admit that I am not who I have pretended to be.

Grumbly Pharisee's ears perk at the distant chortling of a diesel engine. He swivels to see his nephew's truck making its way back down the campsite road. He charges towards the vehicle, cutting across the field where the Holy Spirit is tanning atop the grass that the new-father Villager weed-whacked yesterday.

"What do you think of Vance?" I ask Simon Peter.

"I love him."

"And the directorial team?"

---

23   In Alberta, this is perennially the single largest issue in all municipal, provincial, and federal elections.

"I love Barrett. I love Barrett. I love Barrett."

While the reception of our season has been largely positive, attendance has remained lukewarm—an adjective that may be etymologically derived from the Gospel of Luke. Rumours swirl backstage that the numbers of our first weekend were the lowest in CBPP history. Vance blames the heat, Diabolos blames TV, Judas blames the script, Pilate blames Barrett, Barrett blames nobody because he thinks everything's fine. Personally, I blame Jesus and Simon Peter: the holier-than-thou-ness of the former and the in-over-your-head-ness of the latter.

"I really fear for the loss of the play," Simon Peter says. "If things got so dire financially that we couldn't continue, my heart would be broken."

"Why?"

"The other day, I'm driving home and I'm having this long conversation with God. And I'm whining and crying, and finally I hear the Holy Spirit speak into my heart. And He said, 'Why do you want to be loved?' And there was this whole list of things that came. I want to be loved because I'm a great guy. I want to be loved because I'm a good actor. I want to be loved because I'm an excellent husband and father."

Most of my friends believe the world would be a better place if the CBPP did not exist. Some days, I agree with them. But what do we do with the people who don't agree? What do we do with a man who works as a stucco guy for three-quarters of the year just to afford himself a couple of months to descend into the Badlands and be loved as a great guy, a good actor, and an excellent husband and father: all in that order? What will become of him if he isn't being persecuted but, far worse, forgotten? What addiction will replace the addiction that replaced his addiction?

"I am very much an encourager," Simon Peter says. "I love to encourage people. I love to tell them they're doing a good job."

I recall all the times he called me Prince John, all the times he stared at me so malevolently during brunch that I would eat rapidly and be burdened by ingestion all day, all the times he did not give me a single fucking candy.

"I love to give people the gift of telling somebody, you're precious and you're special."

He has never said I'm precious. He has never said I'm special.

"Every time you've felt a hand on your shoulder, that's me walking by, offering a little encouragement."

I have never felt a hand on my shoulder.

"I love your Herod," he says, and hops off the bumper, jogging to catch up with a couple of Apostles who are preparing for our evening show. But his departure happened so abruptly that there is a chance I misheard, and what he actually said was what I have been hoping for millennia to hear. "I love you, Herod."

The new-father Villager is standing before me. "You and the dog wanna come tubing with me and my uncle?"

Grumbly Pharisee is standing by the truck, a beach towel wrapped around his waist.

Maisy lies in the flatbed, and I sit between the two men in the cab, thighs touching beneath our floral-themed swim trunks. The car radio flashes 12:00. "Will we be late?" I ask.

The new-father Villager shakes his head. "You're Herod. The show can't start without you."

"It can," I say. "It just can't end."

Before he left, Simon Peter told me that during his whole summer acting alongside our celebrity Christ, he has felt as he did when he was an apprentice tradesman. "I would meet a guy who had mad skills, and I would go serve him and work for him. I've spent most of this process feeling way out of my league. Now, I walk out onstage, it's me as Simon Peter. So I'm not really acting."

Grumbly Pharisee turns off the highway and onto a dirt road. At the river's edge, a topless woman is washing a sunburnt toddler who screams with anger. "I've got a little one too," the new-father Villager says, hollering to be heard. "Just a week or so old." The toddler tries to writhe free. "How old's yours?"

The new-father Villager does not wait for an answer. He throws his tube into the current and belly-flops onto it. An osprey dives into the water but does not emerge. Above us, the sun hangs—perfect, merciless—and I feel as if I died a long time ago, the life cleaved from my body, and am still trying to figure what way my soul had split.

‹ SCENE 4 ›

The second week: Friday's show, standing ovation, and I pick up a case of Bow Valley Lager to bring to Judas' trailer, where he and Pilate await. Just before dress rehearsal, Pilate entered the backstage armoury to get into costume and found Judas in hysterics. "B-B-Barrett called my performance last year emotional masturbation."[24]

Pilate wrapped an arm around his friend and made his voice all tender. "Barrett's brain has fallen out his asshole."

In response, the two actors have entered open rebellion. Judas has started inserting himself into scenes in which he was never cast, and today as I splashed around the baptismal pond, I made eye contact with the betraying Apostle as he hid among the onlookers, grinning devilishly. Pilate, too, has become openly insubordinate. During this evening's show, the blood of the Galilean rebels had been mixed with too much dish soap and too little food colouring. After Pilate slew the rebels, pink bubbles rose from their spurting wounds, and he extended his palm to land one of the wobbly spheres on his fingertips, like it was some small and beautiful bird.

They are waiting for me when Maisy and I enter. Pilate is in a grey-green tank top and matching cargo shorts (both a size too small); Judas, in his leather jacket and distressed jeans (both a size too large). I have gotten so used to seeing them in their ancient Israel attire that their street clothes now strike me as costumes—the ill-fitting and decade-late fashions of southern Alberta—as if the two of them are time travellers on a budget, believing they can blend in.

The screen door slams closed as I sit at the fold-down table and turn on my recorder.

---

24   The most shocking thing about this statement is that Barrett knows what masturbation is.

"You fuckin' behave yourself," Pilate warns.

"The play seems to be going okay," I say. "Not just the show, which is kind of struggling along, but the reception."

"We were just talking about that," Pilate responds. "The audience seems to be receiving it well." He frowns at his beer can. "I don't know why."

I tell them my mother and aunt saw the play, and while I withhold my mother's secularity, I press how God-fearing my aunt is. "She's from Phoenix," I say, "but she didn't like it."

"Is she a Catholic?" Pilate asks.

"No."

"I was curious because you are, right?"

"She's a Baptist."

Judas asks what Catholics think about the play's portrayal of Mother Mary.

"I'm a shitty Catholic to ask," Pilate responds, "since I'm not practising or going to church, but I view Mother Mary as an important character. I mean, without her, who knows? I like to believe that God had a long list of other women that He could knock up instead, but if she would've said no, what would've happened?"

The two of them fall into the theological debate of free will versus omnipotence, and I am overcome with missing them. The summer is nearly over, and we will all go back to our unapplauded lives. Where else can you sit in a trailer, as the hour dances onto midnight, drink discount booze, and ponder questions of agency, divinity, and the aesthetic balance of the New Testament? Such a fantastical world we have created, where a grown man can say, without a hint of irony, "Our Crucifixion is lame," and then crush an empty beer can in his fist. Why was God not charmed by our whimsy? Why was such bloodlust the key to Salvation?

Pilate mentions how the other day Abel's real-life wife "had enough of me bitching and moaning, and finally said, 'You're not here for the show, you're here for the people that you consider family.'" He then looks at me. "You're one of those people."

We tap our beer cans together, and Judas mutters, "Queers."

But then, speak of the devil, Abel's real-life wife enters the trailer. Maisy chuffs and then curls back at my feet. Abel's real-life wife is volunteering this year for front of house but has acted in past productions. She says Abel conked out as soon as they got back from the amphitheatre, but she isn't tired.

"Are you okay that I'm recording?" I ask.

She says it's fine, takes a beer, and sits beside Judas.

Pilate, having already forgotten his I'm-here-for-love declaration, starts ranting about how stupid the script is for having him interrupt the bocce ball game that Maisy and I play in Scene 13. "That fucking boggles my mind," he says.

"Why are you recording this?" Abel's real-life wife asks me.

"Because he's going to write about this shit," Pilate responds, envisioning a tell-all about the atrocities committed under our dictator-director.

"Let me ask you this," I say to Abel's real-life wife. "Do you think the script is aware of its historical inaccuracies?"

"No," Pilate says.

"No," Judas says.

"I would play devil's advocate," Abel's real-life wife says, "but I don't want to because I don't like getting yelled at."

"When have we ever yelled at you?" Pilate demands.

"I think it is underestimated how much research Barrett did for this show," she says. "I saw the stacks of books on his desk."

I ask her where she sees that research evident in the play, and Pilate chortles.

"That's a good question," she says.

"It is," Pilate says. "And I want the answer."

Truth be told, I like Pilate and Judas a lot more than I do Abel's real-life wife, but I'm not sure why. She is fun and considerate and nice to the dog. She once brought me an iced coffee without my asking. Pilate and Judas, on the other hand, interrupted our pre-show warm-up today by loudly cheering on a barn spider as it spun and then slowly ate a paralyzed butterfly. In the trailer, they lean forward as Abel's real-life wife waffles, and their eyes redden with arachnid hunger.

I change the subject to something they can all be on the same side for. I mention Pilate's line in Scene 33a: "Be kind to the Jews?!! These people do not understand kindness."

"Do you think," I ask, "there is a charge of anti-Semitism in relation to the Passion play?"

All three of them trip over their tongues as they voice their objections, their utter disbelief of the possibility.

Pilate tries to distance himself from his line, saying, "I think my line is more of a comment on the socio-economic status of those people."

Abel's real-life wife yawns. "Booooring."

I ask her what religion Jesus is. "Christian," she responds, and Judas sighs dramatically.

I ask her who the Jews in the play are.

"Everyone in the crowd," Judas interrupts, not wanting any more flubs on the record.

"Everyone who is not the Romans," Pilate adds.

"But that doesn't come across to the audience," I say. "If you ask people in the audience who the Jews are, they'll say the bad guys."

"I can see that, though," Pilate says. "My problem with the line is that I am very much referring to the Pharisees."

"But," Abel's real-life wife replies, "they are never referred to as 'Jews' up until that part of the play."

Judas swigs his beer. "That's not how the audience reads it, baby."

"But they do that in every Passion play," she says. And she is right. In most Passion plays, the men representing the Jewish establishment are often dressed in dark, ominous colours. In Oberammergau's production, they've even worn horns. However, the Apostles—the first Christians—are always young and handsome, frolicking around in rainbow robes.[25]

---

25 And yes, in this, I include my arch-nemesis, Simon Peter, who—as our last conversation demonstrated—is eminently fuckable.

"So you're saying," I ask her, "that anti-Semitism runs par for the course in Passion plays."

She takes a deep breath. "Oh dear," she says, looking at my phone on the table. "You're recording this."

Why can I never help myself? Why does any sign of struggle lure my appetite? Why must I always join the many-fanged creatures as they devour the weakest?

Because here's the thing: I know it's easy for me (a gentile) to say, but I don't think the Canadian Badlands Passion Play is anti-Semitic. There are definitely anti-Semitic people within the cast (perhaps more per square metre than elsewhere) who leverage the play to voice their beliefs, but the play itself is not creating or even renewing a hatred within people.

An example: Pharisee with Cane is the cast's most fundamentalist Christian. He has thrown ketchup on abortion doctors and called a local naturist club "a magnetized venue for sexual abusers." The Calgary mayor has personally banned him from city hall. Pharisee with Cane is not only anti-Semitic but homophobic, xenophobic, and (considering he always sits alone at lunch with a wide berth of empty seats around him) claustrophobic as well. Yes, there are cast members who, in part, agree with him (Baptizee 4, Midwife 3, Wealthy Herod Guest 2, and even—heartbreakingly—Chuza), but to think that the CBPP's script is somehow responsible for his batshit lunacy is dubious. Pharisee with Cane's moral world is composed of free-floating scraps of logic, unanchored to any central belief. He believes bike lanes are a waste of public money but loathes how the city lets dandelions grow in playgrounds; he publicly protests government grants despite spending his summer performing in a play that annually receives over $50,000 in those same grants; he makes parody music videos that decry the cost of downtown parking while he simultaneously decries the excess of potholes. But the play, I believe, has been a moderating force on Pharisee with Cane, reminding him just how far from the centre he has floated. The cast now treats him as one would a racist

185

grandparent, with begrudging toleration while whispering hopefully about the melanomic moles on the back of his neck.

To label the CBPP as a rat's nest of born-again fascists would be a mistake; not because of any kumbaya reason but because, for the play to be anti-Semitic, the script would need to articulate that, and nobody is able to agree on a goddamn thing this script is actually saying.

My mother thought the play was all about the importance of judicial impartiality. Litia believed the central argument was that geographical proximity to Jesus was the most important part of salvation (which, the more I think about it, the more right she seems). My friend Mikka thought the script was only interested in perpetuating a settler-patriarchy. My other friend Donna focused on the opening scene, where white-robed angels appear along the canyon ridge, encircling the audience: "Was that," she said, "a reference to the Klan?"

Even the CBPP itself is confused. Jesus Christ literally advocates for the first-degree murder of people who dare sell goods at religious gatherings (Scene 27a) only for us to break for intermission and wheel out coolers of bottled water, jumbo freezies, and ice cream treats.[26]

In Judas' trailer, Pilate is ripping another beer out of the box. "My wife said it really well, actually," he says, "Jesus is a celebrity throughout the entire script, as something more than human."

"Is that a problem though?" Abel's real-life wife asks.

"It's a huge problem," Pilate assures her.

"But to somebody else, it's just a different perspective."

"Okay," Pilate says, leaning his head against the trailer's plastic wall, "so, theologically—*theologically*—the Bible states that Jesus was like us in every way, shape, and form. To treat Him as a celebrity, we remove what He is."

"But when Christ is crying," she says, "that's a very human moment, and that is why He needs the spiritual comfort of Gabriel."

---

26 Cash only.

She is referencing Scene 29, in which a kneeling Christ weeps in the Garden of Gethsemane, and Gabriel wraps his wings around Him like a bald eagle guarding her chick.

"But that's not theologically correct," Pilate says.

"But that's theatre—"

"Oh, I understand theatre," he says. "I've been doing this for twenty-four years."

"Yes yes yes," she says, "you done everything for however many years."

Pilate smiles, slows his pace. "The reality is we are not just doing theatre."

"We're not just a play," Judas says. "We're also a ministry."

"You have to do both," she says. "And why am I drinking this piss water?" she adds, shoving her half-empty can into the middle of the table.

Pilate polishes off his own can and starts on hers. "I appreciate this piss water," he says.

"I get the feeling," Judas says, "that Barrett is not interested in a ministry. And it may not be a huge split now, but in a year or two…" He shrugs, drains his own beer.

"It's a slippery slope," Pilate says. "Are we interested in being a ministry or are we interested in creating a theatrical experience? Because 'theatrical experiences' lead to amusement parks in America that are all about the Jesus Experience. Ask my mom about that one."

"There are only so many perspectives," Abel's real-life wife responds. "How can you make the story fresh —"

"Sure," Pilate says, "there's only four entire Gospels —"

"Can I just finish? I talked to Barrett about this. The more interesting people around Jesus are—hold on, let me finish."

"I'm not saying anything," Judas says. "I'm just raising my hand."

"It's like how Mary Magdalene told the story in our John production—"

"Which was terrible," Pilate says.

"Here's my counter-argument," Judas says, his hand now in his lap. "I'm not trying to argue."

"I know, but here's my counter-argument to that idea."

"You walked into this shit," Pilate tells her. "You know how this plays."

"I think it's important to give a different side of things."

"And I appreciate that," Pilate says.

"No, you don't," she whispers. "You hate that."

"Here's my counter-argument," Judas repeats. "If Barrett is exhausted, then it's time to move on."

Pilate says that Barrett is only interested in his own existential crises of faith and is now treading on dangerous territory, where he is revising the Gospels.

I ask where the script has done that, and both Judas and Pilate point to the invented prominence of Simon Peter. In the Gospel of Luke, he's hardly there; in our play, he never shuts up.

"There's a lot more about all the women in the Gospel," Pilate says, "than this script plays. And that is where we fuck up. In typical male fashion, Barrett has decided that the most fascinating character should be a made-up character. He's put a male role dominant when he could have put Mary Magdalene front and centre, or Mother Mary, or Martha of Bethany."

Abel's real-life wife says we're doing that now with Mother Mary.

"No, we're not," Pilate insists. "Everything we're giving her is made-up horseshit that's not scripturally based."

"Why is that bad?"

"Because it's not accurate."

"But who cares? It's an interesting story that—"

"Okay," Pilate says, "let me put it this way: If you were to go to church on Sunday morning and your pastor just makes up a bullshit story and tells you it's in the Bible, you'd be okay with that?"

"That's not what's happening."

"It is 100 per cent what's happening. But my hope is that people who have been moved by our story are going to seek truth, that they'll go and pick up their Bible and be led to a deeper, better understanding of the horseshit we're feeding them."

Judas says that we can achieve a play that's emotionally moving and theologically accurate, to which Pilate agrees. "Barrett has seen better scripts than the one he wrote. Scripts that don't start off with *Gabriel flies in over the fucking audience.*"[27]

"During the John script," Abel's real-life wife says, "the audience evaluations were 90 per cent favourable. Last year, they went down to 60. They're back up at 85. I think what Barrett did is—can I just finish?"

Pilate raises his head out of his hands. "No, I'm listening. I'm just tired."

"It's a double-edged sword," she continues. "Barrett thinks his audience is really smart—"

"I think he thinks his audience is really dumb," Judas says. "He has a style that works for a select group of actors, and maybe that means he's not the best fit for a group of volunteers." He looks at Pontius Pilate. "I'm not going to high-five that."

"Well, I'll high-five that shit," Pilate says, and claps his own hand.

"And this year," Judas continues, "has opened my eyes to the idea that maybe this isn't the place for Barrett."

"I wanna high-five that too," Pilate says and, knowing that Judas won't abide, holds his hand out to me. And, like my arm is being controlled by someone else, I watch as my palm slowly touches his.

A gentle knocking on the door.

Maisy barks, and Judas opens the door to Current Events Villager in her jammies.

"Are we too loud?" he asks her.

---

27   This, I should point out, is not true. Our script starts, *Just before dawn. Lake Genesaret. A distressed SIMON PETER paces on the shores of the docks.*
      The introduction of Gabriel reads, *A MASS OF BODIES, coalesced into a formless blob, enters through the village. In the centre is a winged angel named GABRIEL (see Daniel 10:5–6 for a physical description).*
      Pilate is referencing last year's Gospel of Luke script, which starts, *A chorus of unseen ANGELS makes music in an unknown tongue. The winged angel GABRIEL appears in mid-air.* The script directions then continue to say Gabriel *floats around, speaking to the audience.*

"I am so sorry," she whispers, "but would you mind keeping it down? We can hear everything. And you're swearing."

"Fuck," Pilate says. "Did you want to come in? We're out of booze."

Current Events Villager is real-life married to John the Baptist. She says her real-life husband's head is beside Judas' kitchen wall.

"Do you want me to come over and give him a kiss?" Pilate asks. "I will fucking big-spoon him."

Current Events Villager says perhaps that is not the best idea this evening.

We rise from the table and file from the trailer, which has acquired the smell of a bottle depot. Judas mumbles goodnight and closes his door. Pilate drives home. Abel's real-life wife returns to her slumbering husband. Maisy has to pee and sniffs at length.

Tonight, there is no moon, and the clouds have blotted out the stars. The bathroom's porch light flicks on. Beneath it, Abel's real-life wife is stomping her way to the showers. I hold my breath so I can hear what she is muttering: all of the comebacks she should have said.

When I told Litia that I was surprised at how much I was enjoying myself here, she said, "It's like this place was made for people like you."

"Tall people?" I said, and she left to take pictures of the sheep. Earlier that day, an alumnus of the show said to her, "I can tell you're not from around here with that tan."

How hard it is to give up the little luxuries of privilege, living in a world that bends to my desires before I even know them. "Here," the world says, in a voice like Chuza's, holding out a bowl of grapes, "we thought you would enjoy these." But what's the other option? To stand up to wrongness whenever I see it, even if it's as sprawling and lavish as an empire? An innocent person is brought before me who all my buddies want scourged, and what am I, a lowly tetrarch, to do?

The next day, I am backstage by the armoury, gossiping with Pilate and trying to figure out which one of us still smells like beer, when the Stage Manager interrupts. "Please perform the show as directed," she says.

"Whatever," Pilate replies.

"Not you," she says, and then points at me. "You."

Allegedly, when I am desecrating the baptismal pond, the amount that I splash John the Baptist in the groin has turned gratuitous. "Barrett says cut it out," the Stage Manager says. "We can't risk microphones getting wet."

"Of course," I tell the Stage Manager, bowing my head. Sunday's matinée, when we perform this scene, I instead douse a group of No Liners, soaking them until the curves of their supple bodies show through their smocks.

But the Stage Manager tells me I have to stop that too.

"The audience loves it," I reply.

"Barrett says it takes too much time."

I am about to dispute this (instead of wholesale dismissing it like I do Barrett's other reoccurring note), but I take a breath.

"You get so angry over such little things," Litia once told me after someone[28] had left the milk on the counter.

That fight happened months ago, maybe even years. Lately, we've hardly been arguing at all—but I shouldn't get too rosy about it: half of the reason for this domestic bliss is that I'm hiding in the Badlands and letting absence make the heart grow fonder; the other half is that, on my days off—darling and few—I am so enchanted with the trappings of civilization (memory foam, double-ply toilet paper, a partner that reads the news) that when I see the scissors in the sink, I no longer possess the urge throw them into the garbage with the affected drama of a silent film star.

---

28   Litia.

This tranquility has given me the opportunity to replay past battles. During a recent carpool with Diabolos, I remembered the milk fight, and I asked him what it was like when his wife left.

"The night before, we got into some stupid fight — they were all stupid. The next day, she phoned me at work and asked what time I'd be home. Five o'clock. Okay, we need to talk."

A passing lane opened up, and he gunned it to overtake a convoy of RVs that he'd been tailgating for the past hour.

"I wanted to make it work," he said, "but she was already packed. Kids too."

The passing lane ended, but he still had two RVs to go and continued into the opposing lane, his face empty of all emotion as we sat rigid, unflinching, seat-belted to our sins.

So I'm trying to not sweat the small stuff. This process is meant to holistically expand your attention to focus only on what truly matters. For me, however, it has the unintended consequence of proving my world is comprised exclusively of small stuff: the milk on the counter, the scissors in the sink, the extent to which I can throw water at old men in robes. Hence, I either have to keep sweating it or strut around with the blasé nihilism of an undergraduate philosophy student and admit that life lacks meaning.

But I have learned that the more you believe in God, the less you are afflicted with this problem. The value that the religious find within their lives is best demonstrated by their capitalization of words based not on grammar but importance. And I don't mean just words like God, the Son, and the Kingdom of Heaven; our own program capitalizes "Volunteer Tent," "Arts and Culture," and "Epic Summer Experience." Because when every action has an eternity of bliss or brimstone riding atop it, there is no such thing as unsweatable stuff.

At the start of the summer, I had thought that if I said the words and did the actions, I could blur the line between performance and existence. I didn't have to believe in God; I just had to believe that I believed in God, and eventually I wouldn't be able to tell the difference. But anytime I felt myself sneaking in that backdoor of belief (whether it be during Sunday Worship or pre-potluck prayer or when Maisy and I were hiking the abandoned ski hill and with each step through the tall grass thousands of grasshoppers rose and fell like an emerald surf rolling before us), I would find myself shoved away with a magnetic-like repulsion. "You don't *really* believe," said a voice from behind my temple—which, I suppose, is where all speech originates.

What to do when your spiritual centre rejects spirituality? What if—like the hands of Sienna, the Volunteer Manager—at some time during my prenatal development, the immortal part of me pushed through the amniotic sac to warp and wither? What gives Diabolos the conviction to say that, despite so many of us being born without tongues or eyes or hearts, you can't come into this world without a soul?

Since I have accepted one of Barrett's notes, I figure I might as well accept the other: memorizing my lines. At home, Litia and I sit on the Astroturf of our balcony, share sips of white wine straight out the bottle, and run the script. We get to Scene 33b: Jesus Sent to Herod, when I boot the Pharisees out of my tête-à-tête with Christ. "I just want to see Him," I tell the High Priest.

Litia double-checks the line. "You're right," she says, "but shouldn't that be, I want to see *just* Him? Your way makes it sound like you're blind."

I hold up my hand. "The line is," I say, "what it is."

‹ SCENE 5 ›

Entering the show's final week, the cast's verdict on this season remains inconclusive. Simon Peter is jubilant after each show, scattering five-cent candies freely and generously. Herbalist calls our success nothing short of "Divine." Diabolos recently proclaimed this as one of the best years ever.

Jesus Christ has remained aloof and ambivalent.

But during one of Gabriel's Scotch soirées in the mosquito-netted patio of his on-site trailer, the Apostle James peered at him over his John Lennon sunglasses and said, "I don't remember drinking this much in previous years."

Gabriel poured him another two fingers. "Vance says the feedback has been outstanding, but I had friends that came, and I don't know how much they understood."

Last season's failure was so particularly devastating not because of the show itself but because—during the run—everyone thought that things were fine.

"Vance was all lollipops and rainbows last year," Judas told me in O'Shea's.

"He was shitting marshmallows every night," Pilate added, before the two of them sucked up the last of their drinks: Judas, his ice water; Pilate, his double gin and tonic.

It was only during the off-season that the true extent of the show's collapse became known. The shortcomings were heard first through rumour, then through stage management, then through Vance himself. "This is Luke's Year One," he would repeat during rehearsals; and that motto, in conjunction with his "accidental" destruction of that season's archival video, erased all record of last year from the Book of Life.

But during times of forgetting, remembrance becomes a subversive act.

Backstage, and just as the Assistant Stage Manager gives the ten-minute warning, I spot Pilate, Judas, and Abel clustered together.

"He's here?" Judas hisses.

"No way," Abel says.

"I'm telling you," Pilate responds, "I saw him with my own motherfucking eyes."

"Who?" I ask.

Pilate glances over both shoulders. "Brian," he says. "The director from last year."

⌐ ⌐ ⌐⌐⌐

We meet at a downtown coffee shop. He is wearing a suit, shirt, and tie, all three of which are different shades of olive. He orders a pastry at the counter, but he's so morose that the barista asks him to repeat it several times before she understands. I tell him to go sit down while I finish ordering.

Brian started in the Passion play as one of the paid professionals. He was cast as the narrator for the first year of the John script and kept that role through the script's five-year run. By the end of the fifth year, his performance became so popular that he is still featured on the organization's website. During that time, Brian also mentored the Best Jesus Ever. But all of this could not save him. "After Vance fired Brian," Pilate told me, "he, like, went into hiding. He had to go to counselling because of the trauma. He's still fucking wrecked by it."

When I return with our mugs, Brian is picking the hem of his sleeves. His tie is tight and the shirt's top button pinched. He must be burning alive.

I don't know how to say it, so he does for me.

"I am the guy," he says, "that almost ruined the Passion play."

He buries his head in his hands, and I glance around the café. I am about to offer him a tissue until I realize he is not weeping. He is vaping.

He has concealed the small cylinder in his shirt sleeve. When he's inhaled enough, he breathes the smoke back down the sleeve.

After the success of the John years, the production manager at the time suggested the play take a year off to workshop the troublesome Luke script. Brian, however, urged Vance to let him take the reins, seeing it as an opportunity not only to evolve from actor to director but to evolve the play into the twenty-first century.

"I told him, we can do this and we can make it good—good enough. But I knew there was going to be a mourning for the John script." He takes a long haul on the vape pen, exhaling another plume into his sleeve.

"But don't you think you got the worst Gospel?"

"Not at all."

"Luke is so hard," I say, "and unforgiving."

He shakes his head. "Luke is this great, exploding history that we are all a part of."

Like a lover divorced, he still adores even the ugliest parts about the play.

"That genealogy sequence," he says. "Noah has fifteen seconds. *Fifteen seconds.* It makes you think, *What's my time? What am I doing with it?*" He brings the cup to his lip, and the coffee's ripples betray a tremor in his hand. "We live in both a moment and an eternity. We're all half-divine and half-guttural. *That* is Luke."

My chest swells with the idea that we thespians are sounding our little echoes into eternity, that the genealogy men will be forever lauded as bringers of great truth and vision. Because in sooth, I thought something similar earlier today while performing the sequence. Standing at the back of our first triangle—what Jessica calls our "Mighty Ducks formation"—I noticed that the heat wave had formed symmetrical sweat stains on the back-fat of the Old Testament men, stains which looked like angel wings hidden beneath their shepherd cloaks. And, as per Jessica's choreography, I dutifully placed my palms between those damp vestiges of heaven as we all inhaled together.

Brian drags his hand across the varicose bulb of his nose. "John was emotional redemption. After John, you'd go back to your tent and cry at all the things you felt onstage that night. But Luke..." He pauses, searching for the word. "Luke is intellectual reverie."

But in pursuing that theme, Brian broke the cardinal rule of the CBPP: the audience will tolerate historical revisionism, theological discrepancies, and even a Herod who occasionally goes offscript to flick Christ's nipple, but they will not tolerate boredom.

Brian says, "It's tempting to say it was the script or the Gospel or the actors, but I have to take responsibility for the play I made."

"What do you think of this year's show?"

"I have my opinion, but when people ask me, I say, 'I'm too close to it.'" He takes a drag off his vape pen. "But I have an opinion."

"This year," I say, "whenever something has happened that didn't make sense—like why we needed new boats or why the trial of Jesus takes place in the corner or why the fuck we have the Wall—I would ask Pilate or Judas, and they would always respond, 'Because it has to be different from last year.' Did you see that in the show tonight?"

"Of course."

"And how does that feel?"

"Oh, it hurts enormously," he says. "May comes around, and I start thinking of bentonite and thunderstorms and crucifixions." Another drag off the vape pen. "You're kicked out of Heaven."

Brian is arguably the most successful actor the CBPP has ever employed. He's done far more than Gabriel and Pilate put together. His résumé even beats our *Supernatural* Jesus'. But while so many actors—like our Lord—use the Passion play as a springboard into larger gigs, Brian uses it as a portal through which he watches the lustre of his former life.

"Standing in the centre of that hurricane," he says, closing his eyes. "And in my mind, everything has meshed into one perfect production."

At a nearby table, two young teenagers talk with first-date awkwardness. He is drinking some enormous whipped cream concoction, and every time he makes a joke, she laughs in sharp little inhales while covering her mouth to hide her braces. These happy few, completely unaware that the world will treat their dreams as we do bubble wrap.

Brian is correct that the Passion play is like the wheel of time, not just because of the play's depiction of all human history but because you either hop off at the right second, like the Best Jesus Ever did, or see yourself ground into dust—like Brian, like Jesus Understudy, like Gabriel, Judas, and Pontius Pilate. Like the old Martha of Bethany.

"You hold on to things," Brian tells his trembling cup, "for waaaay too long."

But such is the cost of this Frankensteinian endeavour, of creating something more powerful than yourself, built off your deepest convictions and ambitions, and then praying it does not betray you as you set it in motion. The barista works the espresso machine, and I close my own eyes and can hear the play lurching, heaving, grinding my way.

ннннн

Vance used to work at the local bible college in Three Hills (population 3,212), neighbouring southern Alberta's methane fields. About a decade ago, he was fired under unclear circumstances: Vance says it was because the college was in financial straits and he asked to be let go; Pilate says it was because he tried to start a cult. He went to work as a tile setter and was working on a rural hotel's bathroom when he got the call from a friend on the CBPP's board who asked him to apply for the position of executive director.

In his office, he tells me, "They wanted someone who could manage the company, drive a Bobcat, cook for people—basically walk on water."

I am in his office because I am trying to untangle the Gordian knot of the company's finances, but he's already spun me off topic. He has lectured me on the new sound system, re-enacted his audition for *Oliver!*, and pressured me to join a German opera.

"I have forms right beside you," he says. "We can sign up you and your wife today."

In the corner behind his desk, I spot an ivory-handled gladius, a sword Alexander would have used.

I present Vance with the CBPP's tax forms of prior years. "All years list two full-time staff. But 2016 lists three. Who is the third?"

He reads and then rereads both forms. "That's weird," he says, chewing his lip. "That's odd."

The great peril of lying is that it creates a mirage where vindication is just one sentence away, but pursuing that only lures you further into disaster. I should know. I've spent all summer trying to find my way back.

"Whenever I list full-time staff," Vance says, "I always list me, the Office Manager, and the Administrative Assistant."

In his effort to defend the 2016 return, he has implicated all others. I say, "But every year except 2016 only lists two."

He throws up his hands. "I'm not sure where this is coming from. Our accounting department does all this."

"But this is the only year that lists three."

For a moment, we just look at each other.

"Huh," he says, handing the forms back. "Interesting."

As I stand to leave, I notice a poster of a painting above the gun safe: Nikolai Ge's *Christ and Pilate,* in which the latter demands of the former, "Quid est veritas?"

What is truth?

‹ SCENE 6 ›

After our final Saturday performance, a small group of us are behind
the Jerusalem Wall, brainstorming our evening activity. With only one
matinée remaining, this is the eve of our last day together. Today at
the campground, it wasn't only the teenagers exchanging telephone
numbers and promises to never change.

"Boston Pizza?" Widow with Two Pennies suggests.

"I want to be somewhere where I can be free," Andrew the Apostle
replies, "and I can't be free at Boston Pizza."

Cain nods plaintively.

In the evening light, the sun is gentle, and a cool breeze kisses
the sweat off our necks. It was a good show. Jesus still wrestles with
His lines, but this shortcoming works in the show's favour, affording
the Lord's performance a spontaneity that is both endearing and
empowering, as everyone onstage crackles with the alacrity of not
knowing what will happen next; after our final bow, we exhale with
post-coital relief.

Royal, the artistic director, comes walking through the synagogue
arch, whistling. Regardless of the weather, he wears the same outfit:
a loose-fitting T, an unbuttoned dress shirt, calf-length cargo shorts,
and a hat. Sometimes the hat is a bowler, sometimes an infantry cap,
sometimes a toque, even when it's thirty degrees. He has this swinging
gait, like he's balancing on a pair of railroad tracks. But instead of a
bindle, he now carries a long-stemmed rose slung over his shoulder.

If it seems peculiar that I have yet to mention the artistic director, a role usually so prominent in any theatre company, it is
because—much like the idea of an opening-night party—the CBPP's
understanding of an artistic director is markedly different from the

rest of the world's. For most theatre companies, an artistic director chooses the season's scripts, is highly involved in fundraising, and is the public face of the organization. Here, however, Royal approaches his role from an unexpected angle.

To the outside eye, Royal's job has been sunning himself in the bleachers, where he shoots the shit with rehearsing actors. I have eavesdropped on many of these conversations, and their topics have ranged from the spiciness of that lunch's chilli to the heat of that day's sun to the rapid rate at which Deaf Girl is growing. The only thing these conversations had in common was that they were never about the play. Once, the Stage Manager marched over and thwacked her clipboard against the water cooler. "Excuse me," she said, "but may I interrupt with what we are supposed to be doing?"

Widow with Two Pennies asks Royal, "Are you giving or getting that rose?"

He pushes back his porkpie hat and puts his hands on his knees to stand at her eye level. "I'm not going to tell you," he says, "because then it's a better story."

He congratulates each of us on a successful show. The actors are so besotted by the attention that they scatter in embarrassment. Even Cain, a man who makes a cheese grater seem expressive, has a skip in his step.

I, who am waiting for the dog to finish her evening bone in her sepulchral dressing room, remain. With the others gone, Royal's body slouches with exhaustion. He hoists himself onto the Spice Trader's kiosk and tells me that since he's now sitting, I have to stay and talk. The rose rolls off his lap and into the dirt.

Royal's first encounter with the Passion play was thirteen years ago as a spectator, back when the script was a bunch of ranchers in robes reading excerpts of the New Testament. "I saw the power of the story," he says, "but I was angry at what everyone had settled for."

The following year, he wrote the Matthew script and co-directed it with Barrett. Together, they crafted the most critically and commercially successful show in the CBPP's history. He then wrote the

John script and bowed out of the company at the conclusion of that version's fifth year. But after watching last season's clusterfuck, Royal submitted a twenty-page report to Vance that detailed the many ways the play was relapsing.

"It was really going to be hard for this company to move ahead," he tells me, his feet dangling off the kiosk and kicking the sides. "So when Vance took Barrett and me to EggsOasis that winter morning, I could tell that he wanted the old team that had been successful. I had just gotten the news that my stem cell transplant wasn't working and they were going to start chemo on me, so I didn't know how much I could do. Artistic director is just a title he gave me."

The ambiguity of Royal's position affords him a certain level of clarity—he is far enough away to take in the play's true nature. "I am repelled by Sunday school drama," he says. "If it smells like Sunday school drama, I get my dander up. When you have Gabriel show up, and Dark Angels running around, and we're putting the Devil onstage…" He takes a long, shallow breath and looks up at the battlements, their corners backlit by indigo sky.

I mention the growing feeling among some actors that their faith is being secularized for profit. This sentiment is felt not just by the—as Pilate puts it—"agriculturally based" cast members but the more artistically lenient ones as well.

"There is a belief in the cast," I say, "that this version of the play cultivates a non-religious audience."

Royal leans forward, so close the brim of his hat nearly touches my forehead. "Are you serious?"

"Royal, fuck," I say, holding up one of Gabriel's moulted feathers. "Are you serious?"

"I'm dead serious. Are you saying this particular play has a secular appeal that we haven't had in the past?"

"That this play is a part of a much larger progression towards secularization."

After this evening's performance, an audience member laid into Judas about how Barrett's last-minute rewrite of the play's ending—

specifically the burial and Resurrection of Christ—were not Biblically accurate. But Royal stands behind the cuts.

"It had to go," he says with a flick of his wrist. "That burial scene of Jesus? It was dead. Dead. Cutting that took off eight and a half minutes."

Last week at O'Shea's, Pilate told Judas and me, "When my wife watched the show, she said, 'This is what happens when the Passion play is directed by an agnostic.'" The way he said "agnostic," drawing out the *o* with nasal revulsion, gave me goosebumps.

"But Barrett is Christian," I said.

"She meant Jessica," he replied. "Barrett is Christian right up the ass."

Royal gives me a cross-section of the cast. "You've got all these higgledy-piggledy people who don't fit anywhere, brother. They don't fit. They're artist wannabes who haven't found expression. They grew up in a conservative culture, and they're exploring. That's why I say there's no room for religious people out here, because religious people criticize. And frankly it's too hot."

Royal takes off his hat and wipes his brow with his sleeve. I glimpse his scalp: wispy hair atop skin so powdery I repress an urge to touch it.

He puts the hat back on. "I sometimes wanna slap some of us who volunteer and don't think of these stories. Let's slap them a bit. With a good story—about wine."

Maisy emerges, licking her chops. She stretches, yawns, and takes a piss on the cushion that new Martha of Bethany offers Jesus.

"You can't tell anyone she did that," I say.

Royal locks his lips and throws away the key.

Widow with Two Pennies storms backstage, followed closely by Andrew the Apostle. "If I get any more wet," she says, "because people are getting baptized, I am going to get really upset." She is still wearing her Jerusalem attire, an earth-toned frock now darkened by water.

Andrew consoles her. "Just stand behind me," he says. "I will protect you."

From the wilderness comes a great cry, feral and born-again. Andrew takes Widow with Two Pennies by the hand, and with Maisy alongside them, they charge into the hills, either away from the cry or towards it.

Royal watches them leave. And in the last rays of dusk, his skin turns vampiric white.

The first time I met Royal was during that winter audition. Barrett nodded a perfunctory hello, and Royal, before even introducing himself, said, "I want your hair." He pointed at his beanie. "Then I wouldn't have to wear this stupid hat."

But now I know my hair was just a stand-in. What he truly wants is my life.

His gaze is fixed on the waterlogged footprints of Andrew the Apostle and Widow with Two Pennies. A bat dashes above, and when I look back at Royal, his eyes have softened.

"I was always afraid," he says, "that if I came down here I would get 'religioused' out, that people would be waiting to pounce on me. But these people, they're good people."

I ask, "What do you think about a female playing Jesus?"

"It's funny," he says, "you could have asked what I think about a female Holy Spirit, because that's what we did this year. And believe me, we had a few meetings about that."

I am so sick of this excuse. "Come on," I say. "The leap to a female Holy Spirit is nothing."

"Be gentle," he says, resting his hand on my forearm. "Be gentle with us." And with this entreaty, I know that Royal knows exactly what I am, even if—at that moment—I haven't a clue.

The sun is gone, and a lone floodlight silhouettes him. His baggy clothing morphs him into a shape-shifting darkness. The only definable feature is the hat.

I ask, "Do you consider yourself a feminist?"

He hesitates. "I'm an artist first. But if feminism is telling the truth about something, then yes."

"And how do you think this community treats women?"

"I don't know the community as much as I should. With the chemo, I've been 60 per cent." He rubs his face, and the roughness of his hands sounds like sandpaper against his cheeks. "During intermission, we're selling freezies, and I should be checking on the prices because we're doing a scene about marketplaces where Jesus comes in and says, 'Enough of this crap.' And then we come flying in on golf carts with chocolate bars and pop for seven-fifty."

The CBPP appears to me then to be at the fulcrum of its life—like where most of us find ourselves after having lived a quarter-century, when all the childish coating has peeled off, and we must decide how much of ourselves we'll let the world whittle away.

"What about the future?" I ask.

"Of me?"

"Of the play. Do you foresee a future where the Passion play has fulfilled its use?"

"You know, Oberammergau does it once every ten years. And they save themselves for it. You grow up thinking, *I'm going to be in this thing.* And there's something powerful in that. We put this on every year, and of course there is momentum and community and all that good stuff, but I sometimes think, wouldn't it be fun to do a different story? Is there a time where this story is not relevant anymore or that we're tired?"

He never answers his question. Because my watch beeps midnight, and his body collapses even more, like there is some trapdoor within him that he is falling into.

He hops off the kiosk but loses propulsion halfway and has to wiggle off the corner. "I just want the story to affect me," he says. "From up in the bleachers, I'm watching the wide shot of A Religion. And that's what I thought last year when I visited. I thought, *This just seems like a checklist.*"

He bends over to pick up his rose, and when he uprights his eyes glimmer in the darkness. "You need full truthfulness, and we've had it. We've had it! It's sacred and it's tense and it's everything you want."

Royal is not unaware of the shortcomings of his play (the amateurish cast, the tepid audience, the piss-soaked cushions), but rather he sees these lacklustre aspects as part of what he loves the most:

God. Why can't Noah remember his fifteen seconds of choreography? For the same reason there is no cure for a simple amassing of cells: that God—like all of us—is just making it up as He goes, tottering forward, aiming for perfection but achieving much less.

As we walk out of the amphitheatre, Maisy rejoins us. She is soaking wet.

Royal tells me of a reoccurring dream he's been having about his own dog. "I heard this screaming, and I went outside and Blackie was nailed to a fence post, all four legs. I wake up, but it still tortures me. And I think, why was the impact of that harder than every year we have Jesus up on the cross?"

My aunt told me that chemo does this, gives you fucked-up dreams so that even in sleep there is no salvation.

"They tell you that you have cancer," he says, "and they talk about how many years. So I've been tracking my roads to the Passion play. How being the middle child of a preacher brought me here, how storytelling did, how cynicism did. I'm not going to live as long as most people, so you reflect more."

Even after his voice has become rasped, Royal stands with me in the parking lot and tells me his visions for the future: scripts, special effects, alterations to the set. He has an idea for a Passion play at night, lit only by torchlight and set during Passover, when Alberta is still frigid with early April, the soldiers' chain mail sticking with frost. He brainstorms another about a one-man show of the Gospels. "Maybe," he says, "we need to turn the play on its head. And I think you make it—and this is just me giving you my thoughts—a musical. Because what do musicals do? They transcend."

To the outside eye, Royal's job has been sunning himself in the bleachers and shit-shooting with the cast. But to the inside eye, Royal has the most important job here. He is the CBPP's soothsayer, telling our future—not with any specifics, mind you, but just in the sense that we have one.

Yesterday, wading hip-deep in the Red Deer River as the current streamed through my fingers, I became desperate with the desire to take a fistful of the moment. But I knew—even as it happened—that it was escaping me. And though my heart was in great pain then, I was thankful. Because before the summer started, I couldn't muster up the desire for anything, and it was only my Catholic guilt that spurred me out of bed—that, and the sound of Maisy nudging her leash.

Sunrise is only a few hours away by the time I crawl into my tent. I stare at the canvas, feel the weight depart my body, and listen to the heaving breath of the dog asleep beside me.

That night, the players of the Passion come to me in my dreams. "I'm sorry," I say.

"Betrayer," says Judas.

"Monster," says Pilate.

"Jesus have mercy," I say, and Jesus Understudy says, "No."

"Diabolos," I beg, finding his face in the darkness. "Diabolos." I brush the dirt from his eyes. "Please."

And he opens his mouth, as if about to speak.

‹ SCENE 7 ›

End of summer will mean that Litia and I have been together for six years—which, coincidentally, is the same amount of time the Bible says you can own a Hebrew slave (Exodus 21:2). During this time, I have believed that there is no topic we've left unturned. But I've recently realized that the one thing we've never talked about is the only thing worth talking about: life after death.

If I were asked why this conversational blind spot existed, I'd answer it is because we are of the same opinion: publicly saying, "I dunno," while privately whispering, "Paradise." But one evening and against my instinct, I decided I needed to know. We were on a restaurant's patio during one of my cherished nights in Calgary, and my stomach sloshed with sangria courage. "What do you think happens to us when we die?"

She shrugged. "Nothing."

"Of course," I said, leaning in. "But, like, what do you think *actually* happens?"

She shrugged again. "Nothing."

"Nothing?"

"Nothing."

"But, but…but what about me?"

"What about you?"

"You think Nothing will happen to *me*?"

She smiled, her eyes full of pity. "Even you."

During my subsequent forty-eight hours away from the play, I became obsessed with this question, asking anyone and everyone: friends, family, people at the dog park. I took cover in the anonymity of asking strangers (who were all surprisingly candid) but also forced myself to ask acquaintances, like my volleyball teammates. I waited until the last ten seconds of warm-up before saying, "Oh, Matt—real quick: what do you think happens to the soul after the body perishes?"

And while their situations were all different, their responses were all the same: Nothing.

Nothing at all.

I heard this answer so often that I finally blurted out the only conceivable reply: "Then why don't we just fucking kill ourselves?"

Matt bounced the volleyball. "I think the game's about to start."

"Well, obviously I mean after the game."

In talking with any cast member about their relationship with the CBPP, it's only a matter of time before they say they wouldn't be here if not for the play. They don't mean "here" as in floating down the Red Deer River, or drinking in the Dinosaur Hotel, or tenting adjacent to an outhouse. They mean "here" as in "alive."

In O'Shea's, Judas tells me a story about how, years ago, Simon Peter called him aside and somehow knew the dark thoughts he was thinking and extended him kindness. Pontius Pilate says something similar about a phone call from Simon Peter's Wife: "I say this as someone who has walked away from the Church," he said. "I had the knife in hand when the phone rang." And the idea of telling Pilate or Judas (or Widow with Two Pennies, or Temple Guard Captain, or Dark Angel, or etc.) that they were wrong and it was only pop psychology or a well-timed telephone call that saved them, and that they were revelling in night-light stories to give meaning to their lives, seemed nothing short of evil.

The Bible has its fair share of suicides, seven total: some glamorous, like Samson, who tumbled the Temple's pillars upon himself and his captors (Judges 16:26–31); and some not, like Abimelech, who laid siege to the city of Thebez, only to be thwarted by a woman who dropped a millstone on him, forcing him to demand his armour-bearer hastily stab him in the heart lest people say, "A female slew him" (Judges 9:54). But the Bible's most famous suicide is, of course, Judas.

After seeing Jesus condemned to death, Judas tried to give his thirty pieces of silver back to the priests, but they would not accept it. He threw the money across the floor, left, and hanged himself. This scene only appears in the Gospel of Matthew, so our script doesn't show it, but Judas still bends his character arc towards that conclusion. After exiting his last scene, he is inconsolable for the following fifteen minutes. He sits backstage in the corner, staring at the gravel, his face reddening as he holds his breath to stop from sobbing. Since the CBPP obviously can't afford pieces of silver, we use half-inch washers, but Judas can't keep his eyes off them, his gaze locked on the thirty aluminum circles like they are the gravitational centre of our galaxy, that cluster of supernovas unplugging themselves into black holes.

Pontius Pilate, too, probably did himself in. The Bible drops his character after the Crucifixion, but the Eastern Orthodox Church believes Pilate fell on his sword after becoming crestfallen with remorse. The fourth-century historian Eusebius of Caesarea says he did so after falling out of favour with the emperor. After Pilate's final scene, he, too, doesn't talk a lot. His rancour over the finale subsides, his voice dims, and he slowly changes into his Ukrainian grandmother costume. I once watched him help the Head of Wardrobe as she buckled Gabriel's wings back on. "Aren't these soft?" he whispered, his fingers grooming the feathers.

The winter following my summer in the Passion play, I go into another tailspin. I can't eat, I can't sleep, I can't write. I have these moments where, standing in the kitchen and staring at the bare shine of the empty sink, I am overcome with relief, thinking that I am dreaming. How could I not be? Such impenetrable sadness, one that has a governance all its own. Eventually, the faucet drips, and I realize that I am not dreaming, that this is my life.

A couple of weeks later, around the middle of November, I come home from volleyball to find our one-bedroom apartment overflowing with Christmas decorations. Tinsel grows from the spider plant. Reindeer decals stick to the windows. Our couch is pushed against the wall to make room for my sprawling, two-hundred-piece miniature Christmas village.

Litia is sitting on the floor, crosslegged, marking papers. We agreed not to decorate this holiday, because I was so sad that I couldn't stand seeing happiness. Now, our fifty-square-metre apartment is forty-five square metres of festive.

"Your mother did this," she says.

"Oh," I say, taking it all in, realizing what the nutcrackers, the candy canes, the wooden Santa statue mean. "She thinks I'm going to kill myself."

In the silence, I hear Elvis Presley's "Blue Christmas" playing on the computer.

"Have you tried before?"

"Twice," I say. "Once with a bunch of pills. Other time, tried to hang myself with a bedsheet."

"When?"

"Junior high."

"Both times?"

"Both times."

And both times it was my mother who found me. And it doesn't occur to me until I see the Santa statue, the toll this must take on a parent, that whatever my mother was doing, the dark thought of what I was doing was always hooked in the back of her brain.

Litia asks if I want to talk, but I say no. She goes back to her marking, and I take the dog for a run.

A blizzard has emptied the streets, and I unclip Maisy's leash as we sprint along the lone pair of tire tracks. The wind streaks the snow past us, and the streetlights turn each flake into a star as we sprint at warp speed, careening through the galaxy, hurtling towards its distant corners of darkness.

Hardly a month goes by without me musing about it — and not only when Sorrowvast arrives, but during times of boredom or futility or the neon hollowness of three a.m. and wide awake. And as the dog and

I run through the storm, the odds of making it through my life seem so small as to be impossible. If not now, then surely later, amidst the aftermath of another fresh tragedy. So why not head off heartbreak at the pass? Because yes, there are the wonders of bird feeders, of back scratches, of chandeliers, of the sound of skates on ice, of stretching in the sunlight, of the smell of rain before it falls, and of pasta, and lavender, and dogs; but how are you supposed to mosey on with living, knowing that there is something inside you that does not want you at all?

Yet in those three a.m. moments, I hear the whispering of flames: "You think you know anguish? Just wait until you see our lake." At least, I used to hear it. I don't anymore.

Maisy and I catch our breath on a suspension bridge spanning the river. Beneath us, the water churns ravenously, large white blooms of current, swollen by the storm. The frozen railing bites my palms, and I close my eyes because I am scared.

In the darkness: the old Martha of Bethany. She is standing in the campground, holding her large jar of sun tea, and the light gathers in the glass until she is holding the swirling centre of our galaxy. And the dust hovers around her like planets and asteroids and moons, all as uncountable as the other lives we could have lived.

Long after the final show, she and I meet in a diner and eat hash browns out of a cast iron skillet while she tells me everything I wanted to know.

"I was suffering from a mental illness that impedes my memory," she says. "So I don't remember a lot." When I push for specifics, she replies, "A lot of things weren't handled well. And part of that was my fault because I wasn't open with what I was dealing with, because who wants to talk about that?"

"But why is it your responsibility to talk about it?"

"Because in the back of my mind, I knew it would affect me."

When I was at that Baptist summer camp, on a walk back from the stables, I told my soul-patched camp counsellor that I often thought about killing myself, and he said mine was not a mental illness but a spiritual one.

"And that made me so angry," I say to the old Martha of Bethany. A mental illness places the blame on an incomplete understanding of the mind, that something inside of you has slipped awry and no one's quite sure how; a spiritual illness places the blame on weakness of faith, that if you truly loved God, He would truly love you. I tell the old Martha of Bethany that some actors in the Passion play also blurred mental and spiritual illness. "How would you classify it?"

"I would classify it as a personal illness," she says. "I need God to help me through, I need my therapist, I need my pills, I need my friends. I need a lot of things."

She wants me to know that there were at least a half-dozen people from the Passion play that contacted her afterwards — including Simon Peter's Wife — to check in; that she doesn't feel any anger about what happened; that she continues to believe Barrett is one of the most generous people she has ever met.

She says, "After I got kicked out of the Passion play, I was at a place where I felt that I could excavate and excavate the darkest parts of me and never feel like I reached the bottom. But then I was sitting in a park, and I saw the sky, and the grass, and the mountains in the distance. All I saw was expanse. And I thought, *It's like my soul: it just goes on and on, and it never ends.*"

I recall one of the stage directions from the scene of Jesus healing the Man with Evil Spirit: *to name one's opponent is to claim power over them.*

I ask what her diagnosis is.

"I went through a lot of psychiatric meetings, and the direction they decided to go was dissociative identity disorder, or what used to be called multiple personality disorder. But not all professionals believe that is a diagnosis. A psychiatrist told me, 'If I believed this was a thing, that is what I would diagnose you as.'"

"What do you believe?"

"I don't know," she says. "I can be overjoyed by doing what I love and find deep despair in the midst of that. And those contradictory things can exist in the same moment."

In the Bible, before Martha of Bethany's brother Lazarus died, he was sick for a long time. During that period, Martha sat at her brother's bedside, waiting for the Lord. She had met Him prior, when He dined at her house. Jesus knew that Lazarus was sick, but He did not come. He delayed before arriving to find that Lazarus had been buried for four days.

And yes, the Lord awoke Lazarus from death, but what about Martha? What about all those hours spent watching her brother slip into fever, wrapping his young and lifeless body in cloth, the grief—brick by brick—piling around her. Who can heal those lonesome days? Who can exhume anguish?

The waitress asks us if we want separate bills, and Martha of Bethany makes a joke, and I forget what it is but we turn giddy. It takes us ages to settle, and when we finally do, she looks at me with clear eyes. The smell of grease and coffee drifts in from the kitchen, a spoon chimes against a mug, the ceiling fan slows. Her hair glows into an amber that will keep us perfect for eternity.

But for now, all this exists in my far-off future. For now, I am on the bridge overlooking the river, which churns beneath me, running its long migration, on and on, without end.

This story has never been about the Canadian Badlands Passion Play. It has never been about Herod. It has never been about me. This story is about stories—the ones we tell to make our lives livable. That is the miracle: that we push ourselves like crocuses through cracked earth, all for the far-off belief that we will one day touch the sun.

⬝ ⬝ ⬝ ⬝

The Crucifixion scene requires the entire cast: Christ and His disciples, Pilate and the Romans, the women of Jerusalem, and all the nameless onlookers the wardrobe department can create. But because of the ornateness of Herod's attire, I am unable to switch into something less glittery. I have dragged my throne atop a knoll, where I can peer at Golgotha overtop the backstage's berm without the audience seeing me.

From my gilded seat, I watch the Holy Spirit sing Jesus up the hill, Her voice sirening Him towards fate. Christ is lain across the beam, the hammer ringing off the railroad spikes as His howls ring throughout the audience. And then the crossbeam is hoisted with wincing yanks, and His feet are nailed, and the music swells, and the women bawl, and the Holy Spirit trills, and Jesus releases an unravelling sob.

Then: nothing.

Nothing at all.

The wind creaks the wood.

Once, when we were lucky, a raven cried.

One by one, the onlookers depart, exiting backstage and passing in front of where I sit. Some are solemn, some are shattered, some are locked in thought. Some pluck liberally from the tissue box while some have left it all behind and are laughing, or whispering, or gossiping. All the while, their Saviour is unpinned and lowered to the ground.

And this is how I will remember them. Not entirely sure of the difference between faith and imagination but acting it out anyway. Their open, unabashed, wayward, fervent, unassailable belief that some two-thousand-year-old execution was not for naught.

The scene of me as the archangel Uriel was cut at dress rehearsal. The play was still running over three hours, and certain characters were sacrificed. Hearing this, my heart cringed, but not at the theological revisionism or the last-minute rewrites or even the decrease of stage time, but rather that now Herod will never get his shot at redemption, never get his chance to find what he spent so long searching for.

But Herod's story turns out to be a love story. The Emperor Tiberius was succeeded by his grandson, Caligula, an emperor best remembered for his syphilitic insanity and for making his horse a senator. In a bid for power, Caligula exiled Herod to the Pyrenees. The emperor, however, offered Herod's wife, Herodias, a last-minute olive branch of amnesty and the opportunity to stay in Galilee or Rome. But she refused, and together the two of them walk clean out of the book of history.

After the season's final Sunday matinée, the armoury is padlocked, the Temple entrance boarded up with plywood, and the costumes shoved into Rubbermaids and stacked for tomorrow's journey to the dry cleaners. The entire spectacle fits backstage. Litia drives to Drumheller to give Maisy and me a ride back to Calgary, since Diabolos is staying to close up the campground. She helps me pack my food, find my towel, and roll up the tent. Maisy and I have left an imprint in the grass, the outline of our long bodies the same shape as the holes in a violin's face.

Litia catches me staring. "Are you sad?"

I unplug a peg from the earth. "Of course."

It is dark when she drives us to the amphitheatre. She is dropping us off before she grabs a late-night bite at O'Shea's.

"I'll meet you at the bar" I say, as Maisy and I hop out.

"But you don't have a car."

I shrug. "We'll be drinking, so I can catch a ride with Pilate."

Backstage, the darkness is absolute. The evenings have become short, and an autumnal breeze cuts over the battlements. I unpack my long red kimono from the Rubbermaid to wear over my shorts and T-shirt.

I am meeting Pilate and Judas, plus Abel, his real-life wife, and a couple of others. I walk to centre stage but don't see anybody. "Hello?" I call, and the sound echoes through the valley.

I hear a murmuring in the hills.

"Hello?" I call again.

The murmuring grows, and I cup my ears. Laughter. Maisy and I head towards it.

We walk past the baptismal pond where, during our closing show, I found that I didn't want to leave so instead dipped my fingers in the water, which I spritzed overtop the surrounding wild sage, praying that they'd never turn into tumbleweeds; we pass the pair of fishing boats where I once watched Simon Peter, long after the day's rehearsal had concluded and with the citrus sky behind him, practise miming rowing his boat into the deep water—and my heart ached when, after finishing his self-directed scene, he rowed the stationary boat back to the shore before hopping out; we pass the tomb of Christ, atop which a seraphic tetrarch was supposed to rise but did not, yet there remains some relic that suggests for only a moment he ascended into what he wanted to be: a small chiselling in the painted plywood, declaring that despite all his shortcomings, all his sins, all the many-headed weaknesses of his soul, *Herod was here.*

I enter the audience, to where Maisy once got bored and wandered into the first row, and a hundred hands stretched out to touch her like she was Christ amongst the lepers, but it was the only time she strayed from her blocking, much in the way Persian rug weavers will make one mistake because perfection is reserved for God alone; to where the masses applauded, to where I dressed up a family of Hutterites in my costume as a group of nuns shouted "Us next!" and Mother Superior dibsed my chiffon sash; to the amphitheatre's second bowl, where Royal whisked me away to meet paralytic fans, telling us to say "Cheesus" before snapping our photo.

As I crest the ridgeline, my robe swirls around me, cocooning my body, and I turn to face the silhouette of the stage. Stage left: where Abraham gripped the railing of the second-storey balcony and stared at the clouds and pled "Answer me!" with such conviction that I glanced into the sky; stage right: where Pilate and his horse were led into Jerusalem, and a group of No Liners ignored the emasculating nature of the pony ride and saluted him with a fear so palpable that he, backstage, thanked each of them for their dedication and skill; and centre stage: where night after night, the genealogy sequence was performed dreadfully, pointlessly, and tediously, but somehow this made the play all the better, that the boringness of the Old Testament contrasted with the dazzlement the New—as if to say that once there was no beauty, but now there is.

Maisy and I hike through the hills but find no one. Along the canyon ridge, I trip over the white shroud of an angel. I call out a third time. But now, not even an echo. The breeze stirs up the scent of hay, wet wool, and a wisp of coconut sunscreen. It smells like centre stage after the Nativity. That is to say, it smells like time itself restarting.

The parking lot's floodlight periscopes above the hillside. My cellphone has service but I don't want to interrupt Litia from her meal, so when Maisy and I summit the peak and overlook the parking lot, I am ready for the long walk to O'Shea's.

But beneath the lamppost, the TrailBlazer is parked. Litia is outside, leaning on the door. In the TrailBlazer's shadow, the blue halo of her cellphone lights up her face as she texts.

My own phone chimes.

"Litia!" I shout, as I gallop down the slope.

She squints through the blackness. "Who's there?"

The sand gives way and conveyor-belts me towards her, my cloak outspreading like wings.

"It's me," I say, breathless and alive. "Richard."

CURTAIN CALL

The Canadian Badlands Passion Play did not die. It rose again for another year, marking its twenty-fifth anniversary. According to tax records, the 2017 season's revenue (including concerts of rock and roll) exceed expenses by $3,422. Somehow, the ship stays afloat.

The core directing team remains: Barrett, Jessica, and Royal, who is now in remission. Vance has stayed on as executive director and has moved a stationary bike into his office, outfitting the handlebars with a small desk that fits his laptop. The 2017 tax lists only two full-time staff.

Cuts are made, and the small number of paid performers shrinks even further. But despite such attrition, in the winter of the ensuing year, I receive a cheque from Vance: my travel award from the Sponsor a Performer Fund, a collection taken from the audience to help volunteers cover the cost of gas. Five hundred dollars, which about breaks me even.

On the form letter, Vance includes a handwritten note addressed to me and "Alita": "WOULD LOVE TO HAVE YOU TWO BACK!" I stare at his all-caps handwriting and trace my finger over his gouged signature. I read and reread the mandatory typo on all CBPP correspondence: "It's going to be a great year. s"

Both Royal and Barrett reach out, asking me to revisit my role. Barrett — as accident or as kindness — calls the character "King Herod." Both offers, I decline.

In the following season, many of the cast part ways with the play: Simon the Zealot and his family of six, John the Baptist and his family of three, Barabbas and his family of five, Joseph of Arimathea and his family of six; Susanna, Joanna, and Abel leave as well.

Ten of the twelve Apostles do not come back, including Bartholomew, John, and Andrew. Neither Simon Peter nor Judas accepts a role.

Vance bans Pilate from returning due to "creating a hostile work environment." Pilate and I still go to the bar, he still drives home, he continues to land reoccurring roles on television shows.

Neither Jesus nor Jesus Understudy returns. Jesus moves to Los Angeles to pursue a film career and does not mention the CBPP on His acting résumé. Head of Sound breaks up with Jesus Understudy, but she remains his upstairs neighbour. After overhearing her have sex one night, he decides to move to New York City. At time of writing, no progress has been made on that front.

In an attempt to return to former greatness, the directorial team recasts the Best Jesus Ever in the lead role. The role of Simon Peter is recast with the narrator of the Matthew script, the script that was the Best Script Ever. Fat Jesus, now well into middle age, returns to don the mantle of Herod. No suitable replacement for Maisy can be found.

Gabriel has re-ascended into Apostledom, now becoming John. Diabolos has fallen into Priest 4. The Holy Spirit reprised Her role and is now widely regarded as the play's best hope for a future. The old Martha of Bethany returns as Martha of Bethany and has been granted one of the coveted on-site RVs; when not in Drumheller, she is living in her car. The Passion play has adopted a mental health policy.

But most notably, the Canadian Badlands Passion Play, now renamed the Badlands Passion Play, becomes a musical — more a rock opera, actually. Twelve songs are written and a professional band is moved onto stage, including an electric guitar, keyboards, three percussionists, and a harp.

After two decades of drifting apart, I call Jason D'Souza and ask if he still believes in God. He says he's not religious but he's spiritual. He is now a father of two sons, the eldest of which will be enrolled in Catholic kindergarten this fall. "The Catholic schools have a better education," he says, "but I won't let either kid be an altar boy." Neither of his sons were baptized, but because of plummeting enrolment, the Catholic school board has waved that requirement.

We make a plan to get a beer sometime, and a few weeks later actually do. We talk about income tax, our parents' health problems, and which friends have died because of drugs. Then we give into temptation and play "Remember When": sneaking wine coolers out of my parents' fridge, the school supplies we lit on fire, the time we both illicitly went to a Baptist church and were dumbfounded by how joyous everyone was. We talk beyond last call, until the parking lot is empty, and there is nowhere to go but home. He says he doesn't remember seeing *The Passion of the Christ*, says I might be confusing him with our other friend Dan. He gives similar responses when I ask him about our other times in the pews. Maybe it was Will or Jonathan or Jeff S. "That sounds like me," he keeps saying, "but I don't remember."

Junior high now exists only in memory, in daydreams, in the bar-room shadows. Of course, I wasn't taking notes through any of those years, but what I wouldn't give to have done so. I wish it with a regret so bitter it nauseates. Not so I could revisit the punchlines or the parables or the small treasons of adolescence, but rather to have a written record of how the world looked when we first realized that there were caverns inside of us, reaching like the tunnels of an abandoned mine, burrowing to a depth where it is not possible to see.

⁂

I never used my third and final lie. Though perhaps after closing night, on that final drive home, as Litia steered us out of the Badlands and towards a prairie sky so black it turned purple, I did.

ACKNOWLEDGEMENTS

This is a work of non-fiction, though in some instances I have taken liberties with the biography of Herod Antipas, the location of some conversations with the cast and crew, and the progression of events; for instance, a couple of interviews took place in the latter half of the year, but I have occasionally bumped them forward. Likewise, some interviews were compiled over multiple sittings but have been compressed into one; all interviews have been edited for both length and content. In the bar with Gabriel, the biker selected "Stairway to Heaven" on the jukebox and not "Spirit in the Sky." Led Zeppelin, however, chose not to give permission, calling into question the graffiti on my junior high's gymnasium door (probably written by my brother) that declared Jimmy Page to be God. Thank you to Norman Greenbaum. Where the narrative strays from strict history, my intention has always been to remain faithful to the characters involved and the central story.

The following biographies helped me understand Herod Antipas' place within the world: *The Herodian Dynasty: Origins, Role in Society and Eclipse*, by Nikos Kokkinos; *The History of the Jewish People in the Age of Jesus Christ*, by Emil Schürer; *Herod's Judaea*, by Samuel Rocca; and *Herod Antipas*, by Harold W. Hoehner.

The following non-fiction books were also of great help to me: *Oberammergau: The Troubling Story of the World's Most Famous Passion Play*, by James Shapiro; *Mere Christianity*, by C. S. Lewis; *Jerusalem: The Biography*, by Simon Sebag Montefiore; and *The King James Bible*, by Luke et al.

Thank you to the Alberta Foundation for the Arts, who provided the funding needed to complete this book. I would like to extend my gratitude to the Badlands Passion Play and all those involved for letting me spend my summer with you. I would also like to thank Kealey Storrs for his tireless help, Mikka Jacobsen for her suggestions, Bob "Eagle Eyes" Pruden for never telling anyone that I thought "mustered" and "mustarded" were the same thing, and to Peter Norman for keeping mum about how—when it comes right down to it—I haven't a sweet clue when to use a hyphen. Thank you to Moonbeam Takach for his great love of Christian mythology and *théâtre en plein air*.

With Carmine Starnino all things are possible. An excerpt of this book appeared in the magazine *Taddle Creek* (Summer 2018); thank you to the editor, Conan Tobias, who—as his name suggests—is a hero of both sword and sorcery.

All my love and respect to my parents, Rick and Kelly, and my brother, Tress. Thank you to my soulmate, Maisy, and her joie de vivre, her utter bafflement as to why anyone would want to leave the buffet early.

This book is dedicated to Litia.

Left to right: Judas Iscariot, Diabolos, Herod Antipas, Pontius Pilate, Gabriel (photo: Melissa Mitchell)

Richard Kelly Kemick is the recipient of numerous awards, including two National Magazine Awards, an Alberta Literary Award, and the Norma Epstein Award. His debut poetry collection, *Caribou Run*, was published to critical acclaim in 2016. His writing has appeared in magazines, journals, and anthologies across Canada, the United States, and the United Kingdom, including the *Walrus*, the *New Quarterly*, *This Magazine*, the *Fiddlehead*, *Numéro Cinq*, and *Taddle Creek*. He divides his time between Calgary, AB, and Rossland, BC. *I Am Herod* is his first book-length work of non-fiction.